Finding Our Way
TOGETHER

Bible Study Handbook
Book 3

For leaders of house groups

INTERNATIONAL BIBLE READING ASSOCIATION

Cover photograph   — The Wednesday pilgrimage on Iona
— Maureen Edwards

Editor — Maureen Edwards

Published by:
The International Bible Reading Association
1020 Bristol Road
Selly Oak
Birmingham
Great Britain
B29 6LB

ISBN 0–7197–0938–5
ISSN 140–8593

Typeset by Avonset, 11 Kelso Place, Upper Bristol Road, Bath BA1 3AU
Printed and bound in Malta by Halcyon Print & Design

CONTENTS

Page

These themes match those in *Words For Today 2000* and *Light For Our Path 2000*, so that they can be used by groups who use IBRA's daily Bible readings, but they are also designed to be used by any group at any time.

THE WRITERS

Edmund Banyard A minister and former Moderator of the General Assembly of the United Reformed Church. He is a committed ecumenist and currently edits 'All Year Round' for the Council of Churches for Britain and Ireland.

Maureen Edwards A freelance writer and editor who edits IBRA's *Words For Today* and the *Methodist Prayer Handbook*. Formerly she worked in mission education for the Methodist Church, and served for seven years as a mission partner in Kenya.

Kate Hughes was an Anglican nun for 20 years and then spent 14 years working with the Church in Southern Africa. Today, she works from her home in an Urban Priority Area council estate, editing books and writing and editing distance learning courses in theology. Currently she edits *Light for our Path* and the *Preachers' Handbook* for IBRA.

Martin Lambourne, a Baptist minister and committed ecumenist, has served both in Baptist pastorates and as a Youth and Children's Officer for the Methodist Church. He is now working on projects related to the under-fives, youth work training and family issues as part of his role as Director of Resource Development for NCEC/IBRA.

Joy Mead A poet and writer who is involved in justice and peace work.

Jean Mortimer A minister of the United Reformed Church (formerly Congregational) for 32 years. In 'active retirement' she has taught New Testament Greek in the University of Leeds and is currently involved in theological education via the Scottish Churches Open College in Edinburgh. She is a published writer of prayers and other liturgical material and her research interests are in the area of 'Health and Salvation'.

Valerie Ogden A former member of the NCEC staff involved with Christian education. Since then she has served as a minister with the United Church of Zambia and is now serving in the Wolverhampton Methodist circuit.

Jan Sutch Pickard A writer who worked for 15 years for the Methodist Church as editor of the magazines NOW and Connect, and then moved to the Isle of Iona as Deputy Warden of the Iona Community's work there.

Rosemary Wass A farmer, local preacher, former President of the Women's Network of the Methodist Church, and a member of the IBRA/NCEC Resource and Development Committee.

Acknowledgements

The editor and publisher express thanks for permission to use copyright items. Every effort has been made to trace copyright owners, but if any rights have been inadvertently overlooked, the necessary amendments will be made in subsequent editions.

Useful addresses

Amnesty International (British Section): 99–119 Rosebery Avenue, London EC1R 4RE.

Catholic Fund for Overseas Development (CAFOD): 2 Romero Close, Stockwell Road, London SW9 9TY.

Christian Aid, One World Week and the Council of Churches for Britain and Ireland (CCBI): Inter-Church House, 35–41 Lower Marsh, London SE1 7RL.

Oxfam: 274 Banbury Road, Oxford OX2 2DZ.

World Council of Churches: 150 Route de Ferney, 1211 Geneva 2, Switzerland.

World Federation of the United Nations Association (UNA): Pavillon du Petit Caconnex, 16 Avenue Jean Trembley, Geneva, Switzerland.

How to use this book

This book contains a variety of studies from which to select fresh themes. You do not have to start at the beginning and work your way through unless you choose to do so. Select

- what meets the needs of your group;
- new topics which will challenge you;
- themes which link with current issues.

The aim is that we help one another, through our study of the Bible, to find our way through the complexities of today's world, to renew our vision of God's Kingdom and to find strength to serve.

At the beginning of each study, in the margin, are *keynote readings*. At least one of these is explored in the session. The others are given for those groups who have time for further reading and study.

Preparation

1. Begin by looking at the aim and keep it in mind throughout your preparation and in leading the group itself. At the end of the meeting ask yourself how far you have achieved the aim. Do you need to make more effort to keep to the point next time?

2. Make sure you have read and understood all the Bible passages listed. Use a good Bible commentary.

3. Check that you have all the materials required — paper, felt-tipped pens, candles etc. — as suggested in the notes each week.

A good group develops a strong sense of fellowship and a willingness to be open and honest with each other

What makes a good group?

What is the right number? Between 8 and 12 members is probably the best size. In most cases, a very small group does not offer enough variety of ideas to stimulate discussion, and a larger group inhibits some individuals from participating. If your membership grows — a healthy sign — then it is best to divide into two groups.

A good group develops a strong sense of fellowship and a willingness to be open and honest with each other. But this should not lead to insularity. We are always part of the world around us, the world God made and loves. If we are to grow in faith, that faith must never be purely personal, but able to respond to needs in the community and the challenges and issues of other nations. That is why our studies include suggestions for action, and it is always easier to tackle these as a group.

What makes a good leader?

A good leader
- helps people to feel at ease;
- doesn't start late or let the meeting drag on;
- is sensitive to others' feelings and expectations;
- is a good listener;
- learns from the group as well as leads;
- respects confidences;
- does not allow anyone to monopolize the discussion;
- can accept criticism;
- is not afraid to admit when s/he does not know the answer but will take time to explore the question in time for the next meeting;
- will challenge the group to act;
- enables and encourages others to share the leadership;
- tries different methods;
- cares for the group and builds good relationships;
- makes time for prayer;
- has a sense of humour...

A good leader is a good listener

Other books in this series

Book 1 comprises shorter themes, including:
Jesus — Man of mystery *(3 sessions)*
God's *shalom (3 sessions)*
The Kingdom is for children *(2 sessions)*
The power of prayer *(2 sessions)*...

Book 2 includes:
God's world — God's Mission *(7 sessions)*
The Jesus we meet *(6 sessions)*
Parables for our time *(3 sessions)*
Pilgrimage *(4 sessions)*

Book 4 *(available from September 2000)* includes:
Journey with Christ *(7 sessions)*
New roads ahead *(7 sessions)*
Suffering and a God of love *(5 sessions)*
The power of dreaming *(6 sessions)*

THE MILLENNIUM DAWNS

Study 1 *Vision*

Key readings

Jeremiah 31.7–14
Isaiah 65.17–25
Matthew 25.31–46
Revelation 21.1–6a

AIM

To think about being visionaries for God in the Church and the world, taking inspiration from Revelation 21.

Words and music

Choose a piece of joyful music which conveys hope and new life. Play it on cassette and ask someone with a confident speaking voice to read Revelation 21.1–6a over the top of it. Allow the music to die away and leave some space so that the mood is not broken too soon.

Look!

One by one, place the following objects onto a central table:

- a pair of spectacles, obviously dirty, and a cleaning cloth;
- a small piece of window glass and a chamois leather;
- a box of tissues with one sticking out;
- a magazine advertisement for a local optician;
- a mirror;
- a magnifying glass.

New hope revealed — discussion starter

Plant the idea that Revelation 21.1–6a was a vision of God's world as never before and that it gave hope to people under great oppression. It helped them envision God as being right in their midst, even wiping away their tears, and enabled them to believe that God's goodness would indeed triumph over evil one day.

- In what ways do our Church and world today need the hope of Revelation 21?

Tools for visionaries

Split into twos or threes and invite each small group to take one of the objects from the table as the focus for

In what ways do our Church and world today need the hope of Revelation 21?

further discussion, along the following lines:

Dirty specs and a cleaning cloth
- What issues and concerns 'fog up' our personal, spiritual lenses? Complex sermons perhaps? Tricky moral dilemmas?
- How can our faith and our individual sights and insights be made sharper and clearer?

The glass and the chamois
- Local churches often have a particular window on the world and the world has a window on them. Are we seeing each other with clarity and helping each other to be visionaries?

Tissues
- In the Revelation vision, God wipes away tears from the eyes of his people. In what ways might this part of the vision be mirrored in our day-to-day life and work?

Optician
- In shaping our vision for the Church and the world, whose expertise and which outside resources might we usefully draw upon to help us see more distinctly?

Mirror
- And what of me? Am I a visionary for myself? Can I discern through prayer and reflection what God would have me be?
- Is the image in the mirror clear or fuzzy around the edges?

Magnifying glass
- In our millennium vision, are the most appropriate things being focused on and scrutinized in our churches and communities? Or are the insignificant things being magnified out of all proportion?

PRAYER

Invite each group to replace its object on the table, accompanied by a few words of prayer, or a moment of silence.

ACTION

Within the next few days, find a window or a mirror to clean. Do it purposefully and thoroughly and, in the 'doing', pray for clearer vision in your life and faith.

What issues and concerns 'fog up' our personal, spiritual lenses?

Can I discern through prayer and reflection what God would have me be?

9

Study 2 *Repentance*

Key readings
Hosea 6.1–6
Mark 1.1–8
Luke 15.1–7
Luke 16.19–31
Revelation 2.1–7

AIM

To reflect on the need for repentance in the Christian life, and how best to go about it.

Activity on arrival

Deliberately have the room in which you are to meet a bit messy on arrival — cups to be cleared away, bits on the floor to be swept up etc. As people arrive, let them share in the tidying up. Settle down and offer a word of prayer.

The need to clear away

Talk together about how it was necessary to make space in the room for everyone by clearing things away. Work through the following passages, identifying and reflecting together on the 'clearing away' aspects.

Exodus 20. 1–6	*Rejecting idols*
Mark 1.1–8	*Clearing the path*
John 15. 1–6	*Burning branches*
2 Corinthians 4.16–5.5	*Discarding the body*

What had to be got rid of and why?

● What had to be got rid of and why?

● What is being prepared for?

Inner cleansing

Read the following verse:

It isn't enough to flick on the vac,

And suck up the muck through the spout;

Inside the bag's bulging with nine months of fluff,

So before it gives birth — chuck it out!

What do we think we've cleared away in our personal and spiritual lives but in fact are still holding on to? Talk and share at whatever level people feel comfortable.

The need to turn around

The question is asked of candidates for baptism (or, in infant baptism, of the parents and godparents):

Do you turn to Christ?	*I turn to Christ.*
Do you repent of your sins?	*I repent of my sins.*
Do you renounce evil?	*I renounce evil.*

Traditionally, candidates would physically turn around also. Ask if any in the group remember making those promises, or hearing them made? What impact did it make on them?

Read Hosea 6.1–6 and share life experiences of 'turning' after the necessary 'clearing away' has been done — perhaps from a negative attitude to a positive one, from addiction to cure, from being a couple to becoming a single person (or vice versa), from ignorance to knowledge. At what point did the need to renounce, repent or change become clear?

PRAYER

Place a waste paper bin so that it is behind as many of the group as possible. Distribute scrappy pieces of paper — torn-up paper bags would do — and ask people to identify, and write down, attitudes and beliefs that it is necessary for us to discard and turn away from for the sake of a godly and whole society. (Some members may personalize the exercise more and identify individual attitudes and beliefs. This is fine, as what is written on the papers will not be shared.) After each paper is complete, members can crumple it in their fist, physically turn around and throw it into the bin.

Join hands and let someone offer the following prayer:

Lord, you take our wastelands and plant your roses,
You direct our stubborn feet to turn and walk in your ways,
You dust away our cobwebs with the breeze of your Spirit,
And as the seasons revolve, so you continually call us home.

We turn to you, O Saviour,
We repent before you, O Father,
We renounce evil, O Redeemer;
Remake and revive us we pray.
Amen

ACTION

Find time to read through and think about the words of the baptismal service in your church. Why not talk to your priest or minister about holding a service for the renewal of baptismal promises?

Lord, you take
our wastelands
and plant
your roses

Study 3 *Following*

Key readings

Mark 10.17–31

Mark 10.35–45

John 6.60–71

AIM

To explore the demands of discipleship and find encouragement to stay the course.

Complete the sentence...

Ask each person to complete the sentence:

'Recently I've been finding it hard to...'

Answers could range from '...get up in the morning' to '...understand the doctrine of the Trinity'! See if you can categorize the responses under these headings:

● hard to understand intellectually;

● hard to put into practice.

Naturally some responses may have the element of both. Christian discipleship encompasses both demands, as the following key readings show.

Discipleship demands understanding

Read John 6.60–69.

Do we feel out of our depth and a bit suspicious of the word 'theology'?

By the time John's Gospel was written, the early Christians would have established patterns of eucharistic worship, but their practice of eating 'flesh' and drinking 'blood', in the form of bread and wine, was regarded as highly controversial and complex. Chapter 6 is devoted to a theological explanation of this issue through the mouth of Jesus, but by verse 60 many disciples are still as confused as ever: 'This teaching is difficult; who can accept it?' they say.

Invite people to be honest about the so-called 'intellectual' side of their faith:

● What do we find difficult to understand in the Bible? In sermons?

● How well do we stand up in a discussion with a Jehovah's Witness?

● Do we feel out of our depth and a bit suspicious of the word 'theology'?

Explore ways to increase understanding and confidence. Resist just focusing on the negative.

Discipleship demands action

Read Mark 10.17–31.

Encourage discussion about the new demands made on this young man. His understanding of the commandments is undisputed, but the greater demand made of him by Jesus moves from knowledge to action. Discuss the practical, sacrificial demands of discipleship that face ordinary Christians day by day.

Discipleship diagram

On a large sheet of paper, draw the diagram below. As a way of summarizing this study, in the 'head' circle, write down some of the intellectual demands of discipleship that the group identified, and in the 'hand' circle, some of the practical sacrificial demands. Decide together what to write or draw in the segment where both circles meet.

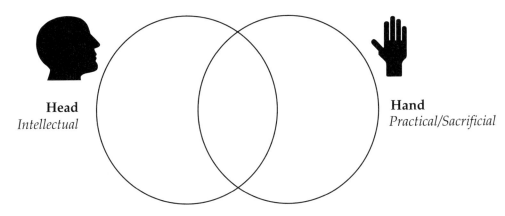

Head
Intellectual

Hand
Practical/Sacrificial

PRAYER

Sing or say, quietly and reflectively, the hymn 'Father, hear the prayer we offer'.

ACTION

Face up to the aspect of the Christian faith that you find mentally challenging by reading a book, talking to your minister or using another resource. Alternatively, commit yourself to a piece of practical, sacrificial discipleship that won't come easy, and tackle it in faith.

Study 4 *Proclaiming the good news*

Key readings

Mark 1.14–20
Mark 6.7–13
Luke 4.16–30
Romans 1.1–17

AIM

To realize our calling to live and speak the gospel in our own day and age.

And here is the news...

If the time of your meeting coincides with a news bulletin on radio or TV, listen to or watch it (or part of it) together. Alternatively have enough assorted newspapers and newsy magazines for one between two.

Read Luke 4.16–19 and identify the different aspects of Jesus' ministry that he speaks about, with reference to Isaiah 61.1–2. Based on the passage, write a different 'good news' heading on large, separate sheets of paper, along the lines of:

Do we assume that there is no good news to be proclaimed for the Kingdom today because we are so often fed with the negative?

- good news for the poor;
- release to the captives;
- recovery of sight to the blind;
- freedom for the oppressed;
- salvation for God's people.

News gathering

Reflect on the reports from the news bulletin and/or spend time looking through the papers. Select stories that would fit the headings, e.g. the story of a refugee family being well received might come under 'freedom for the oppressed'. The story of a politician apologizing for the error of his former ways might go under 'recovery of sight to the blind!' Cut and stick the stories onto the large sheets, or summarize them briefly in writing.

The time is now

Jesus said, 'Today this Scripture has been fulfilled in your hearing.' Listeners in the synagogue were amazed. The age-old prophecy suddenly had urgent, contemporary meaning. Look together at the six sheets of 'good news' you compiled from contemporary sources. Was the group surprised to find such material? Do we assume that there is no good news to be proclaimed for the Kingdom today because we are so often fed with the negative? Talk about how to identify and proclaim the good news in our day and time.

Don't delay
One of the biggest hindrances to living and speaking the gospel in the world is the attitude that says the time is not right. Tell this story:

'At a celebration of the 50th anniversary of the World Council of Churches in 1998, Archbishop Desmond Tutu paid tribute to the organization's role in the movement which led to the end of apartheid. Yet when the WCC's Programme to Combat Racism was launched, many said the time was not right. They claimed that the Churches were not ready to fight racism in their structures and society. Although much remains to be done to fight racism, we can see the results of a change of attitude, behaviour and policies — good news for many.'

Simon Oxley, 24.1.99

Act now
Challenge the group to identify and work immediately on a specific area for change in their church's life, their neighbourhood, or their community: e.g. that notice board rotting outside the front of the church with a torn poster on it; that day centre which urgently needs extra helpers... The rallying cry should be, 'We must work on this NOW so that good news may be proclaimed.' Make an action plan. Apportion responsibility. Decide on a time-scale and a deadline for reporting back.

PRAYER and WORSHIP
Use the song, 'God's spirit is in my heart...' or another that expresses the theme of good news. Offer to God your decision to act and pray for wisdom and commitment to the task.

One of the biggest hindrances to living and speaking the gospel in the world is the attitude that says the time is not right

Study 5 *Deliverance from evil*

AIM

To investigate evil through biblical and modern day examples, and reaffirm our desire to reject it and choose the good.

Recognizing evil

The Collect at the end of Evening Prayer in the Church of England says,

> *'Lighten our darkness, Lord we pray, and in your mercy defend us from all perils and dangers of this night.'*

What do we understand by 'perils', and 'dangers', in our day-to-day lives? Share and discuss.

The perils of prophecy

Read 1 Kings 22.1–4 dramatically. You will need a narrator, King Jehoshaphat of Judah, the King of Israel, 400 prophets (everyone!), Zedekiah, a Messenger and Micaiah. Enjoy play acting the story.

Discuss Micaiah's choice; to go along with the 400 false prophets and please the King, or to speak the Lord's word, however unpopular that might be *(verse 14).*

● In what ways do believers today come up against the perils of prophecy?

● How can we tell a genuine prophet from a false one in today's world?

How can we tell a genuine prophet from a false one in today's world?

The dangers of deceit

Read Mark 6.14–20.

Here are some evil elements in Herod's tangled web of deception:

— abusing power to arrest an innocent man;

— failing to listen to godly and sensible advice;

— allowing himself to be manipulated;

— bearing a grudge;

— making rash promises;

— allowing evil to be done through cowardice.

React to the 'perils and dangers' that Herod found himself

caught up in.

- Do you find him to be more 'evil' than the average flawed human being?
- Imagine you had been Herod's spiritual adviser. What would you have said to him?

Evil options
Explore the meaning behind the following popular statements and give examples of their truth, or otherwise:

— 'O what a tangled web we weave, when first we practise to deceive!'

— 'Evil prospers when good people do nothing.'

— 'Hear no evil, see no evil, speak no evil.'

PRAYER
Offer everyone a decent pen and piece of paper and encourage them to write out the words of the Lord's Prayer attractively, taking time over it, and possibly drawing a border decoration.

Ask for God's help in confronting evil in the world

Spread out the prayers in a circle in front of everyone and have a time of open intercessions to ask for God's help in confronting evil in the world and promoting love, goodness, justice and peace. The following bidding and response can be used at the end of each prayer:

Lord, deliver us from evil

And urge us to choose the good.

ACTION
If you are not already in touch with a charity or organization that deals with a particular 'evil' in society (e.g. child abuse, neglect of human rights), write for their materials and consider how you might work with them, even in a small way, to counteract evil in the name of Christ. Possible organizations might be:

— NCH Action for Children;

— ACT — Association of Christians Against Torture;

— Christian Aid...

Study 6 *Renewal*

Key readings

Isaiah 40.21–31
Mark 1.29–39
Ephesians 1.15–23

AIM

To see the need to take a fresh look at familiar situations, with biblical guidance, in order to renew the Church.

A story to share

Some miles away, off the main tarmac road that runs through Zambia's Copperbelt, the Mupeta family waved goodbye to the driver and the pick-up truck that had brought them safely to their new home. As the truck disappeared in a cloud of red dust, they started to unpack; pots, pans, a mattress or two, and soon a charcoal fire was lit to cook the beans for dinner. The Mupeta family were proud of their small but fertile piece of farmland and the basic house they had managed to build on it, scrimping and saving for many years from the wages Dad had earned as a government clerk. Now they would settle, keep some ducks and pigs if the Lord blessed them, grow some maize and, most important of all, do something that they were sure God wanted them to do: build a church.

There was no Christian community in the area but the family was determined there soon would be. Dad had been an elder in his last congregation, Mum a staunch member of the Women's Fellowship, and all the children had been through Sunday School or had sung in the choir. Within two weeks, the family had cleared a piece of scrub land, with their bare hands, arranged stones for sitting on and made a roughly hewn pulpit out of small tree trunks. On the following Saturday, they started the long trek from farm to farm, through several small villages, inviting neighbours far and near, 'Come. God is calling you! Come and help us build a church in this place.'

'Come. God is calling you! Come and help us build a church in this place.'

Less than 12 months later, a congregation of over 60 men, women and children was meeting regularly. There was a small choir, a Men's and Women's Fellowship, a Sunday School and a preparation class for baptism. Where once had been scrub land, with only the voices of birds and crickets to be heard, there stood a building of mud bricks and a grass roof, resounding week by week with Christian voices raised in song. There had been no official decision taken to plant a church in that area. No one had drawn up

18

plans, consulted architects, applied for funding or asked permission from the Bishop. The ground and the area had been claimed for God by a Christian family whose work was enriching and renewing the lives of their neighbours.

Share your reactions to the story.

● What are our experiences of new life or renewed life in the church situations that we know?

● What encourages new life and renewal?

● What hinders new life and renewal? Make a list.

Time to move on
Read Mark 1.29–39 and talk about the following points:

● Jesus and his disciples were 'successful' in that place; they healed, attracted large crowds and brought comfort to many. It may have been tempting to stay.

● Jesus seeks guidance from God through quiet prayer.

● Jesus discerns that it is time to move on. 'Let us go on to the neighbouring towns.' *(verse 38)*

● What is your experience of the Church's ability to move on?

● Can anyone share another contemporary story of Christians, like those in Zambia, who moved on in faith?

What hinders new life and renewal?

PRAYER
_____

Sing 'One more step along the world I go', or another song of new life and renewal. Offer this or another prayer:

Open our eyes, Lord,
to see the place where you have put us
as fertile soil for your purposes.

Teach us to discern and plan,
toil and risk,
believe and pray,
so that our lives may be agents of renewal.

For your Kingdom's sake. Amen

ACTION
_____

Find out more about church planting and building in the developing world — there are some tremendous stories of renewal to inspire the most weary and cynical of congregations!

NOTES
BY
EDMUND
BANYARD

KEY WORDS OF FAITH

Study 1 *You are called*

Keynote readings

2 Kings 5.1–14
Jeremiah 1.4–19
Isaiah 43.1–7
Acts 26.4–18
1 Timothy 1.12–19

Can you think of any people you would see as instruments the Almighty uses?

AIM

To consider what being 'called of God' actually entailed in various situations and to ask what it might mean for us.

Way in

Briefly compile a short list (not more than ten names) of people, past or present, you would agree had been 'called of God' and then put it aside for later reference.

Two young people

The familiar story of the healing of Naaman *(2 Kings 5.1–14)* begins with an Israelite slave girl chatting with her mistress. Slave she may be, but she shows a real concern for her master and absolute confidence that Elisha, a prophet in her homeland, could cure him. There is no hint of special revelation here; she just talks of what she knows and believes. Great events follow but she has no part in them.

The young Jeremiah on the other hand is burdened with a sense of call *(Jeremiah 1.4–19)*. He would escape it if he could, but he cannot. Instead he becomes ever more aware of the enormity of the task laid upon him.

● Would you consider the Israelite girl 'called'? If so, what do you think it was about her which made her a tool which God could use?

● Can you think of any people you know who, though they might laugh at the suggestion that they were called of God, you would see as instruments the Almighty uses?

● Jeremiah's sense of 'call' continued throughout his long life but he never gained much respect from his contemporaries. Is there anything we learn about him in this passage which suggests why later generations have regarded him as one of the greatest of the prophets?

The call of a people

It was towards the end of a long period of exile, and Israel was down and out, when a prophet gave this ringing reassurance *(Isaiah 43.1–7)* that they were a specially chosen people, called of God. No doubt the whole nation would have been glad enough to have been the special recipients of God's favour. What they were unable to accept was that being called of God meant added responsibilities towards others, being servants, not masters. Today it is the Church in all its manifestations that is called to be a servant people.

● What do you consider some of the successes of the Church in being what it is called to be?

● What would you regard as some of its saddest failures?

● In areas where you can make an input (e.g. your own congregation) do you recognize ways in which you could be more open to God's call?

The call to witness

Paul had had a dramatic conversion experience and we find him *(Acts 26.4–18)* a prisoner with a capital charge hanging over him. But he was more than ready — in the hope of influencing others, be they high or low — to give an account of how he came to be called.

● Few will have had such a shattering experience as Paul, but how important is it that we should, each and every one, be ready to give an account of where we stand and how we reached that position?

He who calls sustains

Paul draws on his own experiences to encourage Timothy *(1 Timothy 1.12–19)*. It is quite clear that Paul doesn't expect Timothy to have an easy time any more than he has had. Timothy is to 'fight the good fight with faith', but Paul writes of being made equal to the task, receiving grace and the knowledge of sins forgiven. For him these are so significant that he breaks into a great 'Gloria' *(verse 17)*.

● What particular difficulties do you face in trying to live out a Christian life?

How important is it that we should be ready to give an account of where we stand and how we reached that position?

21

● Do you think Timothy would have found Paul's words encouraging? Do you?

In conclusion
Look again at the list you made at the beginning. Would you want to alter it, maybe broaden it, in the light of the study?

PRAYER

From being blind when we should see,

deaf when we should hear,

and unwilling to break out of cosy routines;

Good Lord, deliver us.

ACTION
Make a little space in the next few days to think seriously about God's call and what the Almighty might be asking of you at this time.

Study 2 *You are forgiven*

Keynote readings
Isaiah 43.18–25
Psalm 41
Mark 2.1–12
2 Corinthians 5.11–21
Romans 4.1–12
2 Corinthians 1.18–22
John 8.1–11

AIM
To ask what it means that we are forgiven and in what way this forgiveness requires us — in our turn — to be forgiving.

Way in
Take one or more examples of deep-rooted conflict from the current news and ask each member of the group in turn which they think it would be the more difficult for the protagonists to do:

— To say they will forgive;

— To admit that they need to be forgiven.

Accept your need of forgiveness, and know that you are forgiven
'Stop brooding over days gone by', cries Isaiah *(Isaiah 43.18).* You can image people moaning, 'Why should it have happened to us? It wasn't our fault', failing to acknowledge that there was a great deal wrong in their living. They were missing the glorious message that God was ready to forget all that was bad in the past and start

them on a new road. The psalmist *(Psalm 41)* on the other hand, in his suffering, acknowledges sin but with confidence in a forgiving, saving God.

● Can we experience forgiveness without some form of confession, i.e. can we be forgiven for sins we won't acknowledge?

Forgiveness liberates
Isaiah was declaring God's forgiveness as clearing the way for exiles to make the considerable effort which would be required to return to their homeland. The words of the psalmist and the words of Jesus in the Markan Gospel story link forgiveness with restored health.

● On one occasion Jesus specifically asks a cripple, 'Do you want to get well?'*(John 5.6)*. Forgiveness often leads to new challenges, e.g. a journey into the relatively unknown for the exiled Jews, or the need for a cripple to get active after a long period of dependence. Reflect on the tendency to say, 'Leave me as I am'. Think of other examples. It was being able to believe that he was forgiven, whatever sin it was that lay heavy on his heart, which enabled the paralysed man to get up and walk. Do you believe that the knowledge of God's forgiveness should liberate us for more positive living?

Reconciled to proclaim reconciliation
Paul begs his readers *(2 Corinthians 5.11–21)* to be reconciled to God that they may be messengers of reconciliation to the whole world, whilst in another passage *(Romans 4.1–12)* he employs a legalistic argument to show that this reconciliation is indeed for the whole world and not merely for Israel.

● Are there people to whom you would find it very difficult to proclaim the message that God reaches out through Christ with a universal offer of reconciliation, of forgiveness?

● Look again at 2 Corinthians 5.19–20. How important do you think these words are? Does the church you know take them sufficiently seriously?

Can we be forgiven for sins we won't acknowledge?

Do you believe that the knowledge of God's forgiveness should liberate us for more positive living?

Is there room and need for Christians to offer more positive help to folks wanting to make a new start?

And after you're forgiven?

The remarkable incident recorded in John 8.1–11 prompts the question: What happened next? Jesus had saved the woman from a violent death, but were the men involved sufficiently shamed to leave her alone? Was some safe haven found for her where she could begin life afresh? We cannot know, but we are reminded that the forgiven may still have a hard road ahead of them.

● What means do you know of in your area to help people make a new start after they have brought trouble on themselves?

● Is there room and need for Christians to offer more positive help to folks wanting to make a new start?

PRAYER

In a period of quiet let each remember some of the things they have been forgiven and thank God. After a suitable time say the Gloria together.

ACTION

If there are any rifts in your own relationships caused by injuries you have found it hard to forgive, or hurts that others feel deeply, commit them again to God, listening for any fresh word which may be spoken in your heart.

Study 3 *You are loved*

Keynote readings

Hosea 2.14–20
Hosea 11.1–9
Psalm 103.1–13,22
Mark 2.13–22
Mark 5.21–43
2 Corinthians 3.1–6

AIM

To think again of what it means for us that 'God is love', and what it means for the world.

Way in

List different ways in which the word 'love' is used, e.g. 'It was love at first sight'; 'I do love baked beans'. When your list is complete, go through it and mark which phrases use 'love' in a way compatible with a Christian understanding of the word.

God — the loving, dependable husband and father

Though the unfaithfulness of Hosea's wife caused him great pain, he found that he couldn't stop loving her and that he longed to have her back. This led him to reason, 'If my love is like that, how much more is God's love for his people.' Thus we find him *(Hosea 2.14–20)* hearing God speaking in terms of a loving husband putting the past behind and making a solemn covenant with his wife for a restored relationship. Later *(Hosea 11.1–9)* the image changes to the father longing for his wilful son. We might compare this to the father Jesus pictured eagerly waiting for his lost son to return *(Luke 15.20)*.

● Have you had an experience of people you loved deeply hurting you, or letting you down?

● Hosea found he still loved under those conditions and learned that God did the same, only so much more. How would you try to describe such love?

God's loving kindness acknowledged
In Psalm 103 we have a great hymn of praise for the many blessings we receive and the father/child image appears again *(verse 13)*.

● The psalmist is counting blessings with great joy. If you were writing the psalm today, what additional blessing would you want to include in this list?

Love reaches out in unexpected ways
As a teacher/preacher newly on the scene, Jesus would have been expected to be careful about where and when he chose to offer friendship; he is, but not in the way people were used to *(Mark 2.13–22)*. Jesus goes out of his way to make friends with outsiders who are despised by 'good upright people'. He is showing that God's love reaches out to all and that this is something to rejoice about.

● Discuss who, outside your circle, you would be willing to reach out to in friendship. Where might you draw the line?

● Where do you think God draws the line?

Love has time for everyone
Jesus is on his way to see a sick child and, as it happens, the child of a family quite important in the community *(Mark 5.21–34)*. With a crowd pressing in and jostling him, he is nevertheless aware of someone in real need touching him. He stops and for the moment gives all his attention to

Jesus goes out of his way to make friends with outsiders who are despised by 'good upright people'

Where do you think God draws the line?

25

the woman. Only when he has satisfied her need does he resume his journey and, though most thought he was too late, he was still in time *(Mark 5.35–43)*.

● Can you think of times when God may have come to you in the person of the one who interrupts when you are busy?

● How hard do you find it to make time for the person who breaks in unexpectedly and still get done what needs to be done?

Can you think of times when God may have come to you in the person of the one who interrupts when you are busy?

Reflecting the love of God

Read 2 Corinthians 3.1–6. Paul doesn't mention the word 'love' here, but love colours every word he writes. Paul is having problems with this church and we can see how he feels personal agony. Had he not established them? Are they not part one of another in Christ? Here it is Paul. It could have been Jesus — 'O Jerusalem, Jerusalem...' *(Matthew 23.37)*. And through these human cries comes the cry of God.

● That God loves us and cares what happens to each and every one of us is central to the Christian gospel. Share with one another some of the times when you have been able to make this truth your own — to hold on to it in good and bad times alike.

● Does the knowledge that you are held in love help you to go on loving when there is a strong temptation to give up?

PRAYER

God beyond time
yet meeting us in time;
even as we seek to clear a way for you
through the wilderness of our living
you are already at our side.
You are the God who broke into history,
you are the God of the present moment
and you are the God who is yet to come.
You were in our yesterdays,
you are in our 'now'

and you will be in our tomorrows.
Thanks be to you,
God ever present,
God of all generations,
for your unfailing love.

ACTION
Try to make a point at least once in each of the next few days of saying to yourself, 'God loves me just as I am. God loves ME.'

Study 4 *You are changed*

AIM
To look beyond the way we live day by day and to ask what more our Lord may require of us, and whether he is looking for any change.

Way in
What are some of the most significant changes that have occurred during your lifetime? Compile a short list as a background to this study.

'Rend your hearts and not your garments'
Joel *(2.1–2, 12–17)* is addressing people who may well know that things are badly wrong in the life of their nation and yet fail to face the fact that they ought to get involved in putting wrongs to right. The image of rending the heart *(verse 13)* means acknowledging some responsibility for what is happening and an awareness of the need for penitence.

● What do you think to be the worst ills in your society?
● Do you feel that in any way you share the guilt for some of the things that are wrong; if so, what should you be doing about it?

'Against you only have I sinned'
Jesus roundly condemns those who seek to keep to the letter of the law whilst avoiding its intentions *(Matthew 23.23–28)*. In contrast, the psalmist's very closeness to God *(Psalm 51)* makes him only too aware of how far short he

Keynote Readings
Joel 2.1–2, 12–17
Psalm 51.1–17
Matthew 23.23–28
Isaiah 58.1–12
2 Corinthians 5.20b
to 6.10
Philippians 3.1–11
Colossians 3.5–11

What do you think to be the worst ills in your society?

27

Does it make sense that a committed Christian might be more aware of sin than one who never enters a church?

falls of what he seeks and strives to be.

● Does it make sense that a committed Christian might be more aware of sin than one who never enters a church?

● Do you think confession brings us closer to God? In what ways might it lead to change for the better?

The offering of worship is not enough

We find Isaiah *(58.1–12)* declaring that God takes no delight in worship unless the worshippers are following it up in the way they live their everyday lives. Instead of organizing special services and fast days, he cries: Stand out against injustice, feed the hungry... Look closely at verses 6–7.

● Isaiah is very specific in the call to his own day. What particular evils might he have focused on in our world?

Triumph in adversity

When we turn to 2 Corinthians 5.20b–6.10, in which Paul sets out a catalogue of sufferings, we can't help but note a sense of overflowing joy, finding its climax in that amazing phrase 'penniless, we own the world'. Paul was certainly somebody whose life had been dramatically changed by the gospel.

● How do you understand Paul's cry *(6.10)*, 'Penniless, we own the world'?

● Is being called to share in God's work, as Paul felt called, something to be prized, come what may?

Pilgrims to the end

Our theme has been 'You are changed', but it has been very clear from the Bible passages which we have been discussing that even if we are, it is not a once-for-all experience. We need to be open to further change as long as we continue our earthly journey. In Philippians 3.11, Paul makes it clear that he is still a pilgrim 'in the hope of somehow attaining...' whilst in Colossians 3.5–11 he stresses that the 'new nature' has to be constantly renewed.

● How difficult do you find this need to be a pilgrim people, ready to face change, willing to be on the move?

● What constants are there that do not change?

PRAYER

May my mind ever be open to fresh revelation,
to new understanding of ancient truth.
May my heart be as ready to trust my God
as a newborn child is to trust a loving parent.
May I, unfettered by anything in the past,
be ready to grasp and accept
whatever the future may hold for me.
May I be willing to be changed.

ACTION

During the next few days take a little quiet time to look back and consider how much you see your life so far as a pilgrimage, a progression involving a succession of changes.

How difficult do you find this need to be a pilgrim people, ready to face change, willing to be on the move?

29

NOTES
BY
JAN S PICKARD

READINGS FROM THE GOSPEL OF JOHN

Study 1 *Turning to the light*

Keynote readings

John 1.1–18
John 3.1–21
John 5.1–29
John 7.1–31

AIM

To explore how we encounter Jesus in our lives today.

Try a simple experiment

Ask the group to hold this or another book up against the window or a lamp so that it blocks out the light rather than being illuminated by it.

Or ask someone to sit with her back to a window, or lamp. Continue with the study but, after a while, ask her how this has affected her.

Read John 3.21.

Encounter

Imagine that you are one of the following people:

● Nicodemus *(John 3.1–21)*;

● the man who had been ill for 38 years *(John 5.1–29)*.

How would you describe to your friends your encounter with Jesus?

Half of the group could take the part of Nicodemus and discuss together how he might have felt, while the other half do the same with the disabled man. In pairs, across the groups, compare these experiences.

Coming to the light

Again, read aloud John 3.21.

● What might these words mean to Nicodemus and the man who had been ill for 38 years?

● What do they mean for you?

● How do you — or could you — 'come to the light'?

● In what ways do you think you make it harder for other folk to glimpse God?

● How could your actions and way of life change to

In what ways do you think you make God harder for other folk to glimpse?

enable others to see God more clearly?

Ask the group individually to jot down several personal action points so that they can refer back to them over the next few weeks.

These jottings can remain purely personal, or you could help each other to put them in order of priority.

PRAYER

Jesus, just as you met, enlightened,
encouraged and challenged
those who stumbled across you or sought you out,
so today, every day, we can encounter you
at work, at home, among our neighbours.
Help us to recognize you and to respond
and may we show your love and light to others. Amen

Study 2 *Signs of God's love*

AIM

To look at one Gospel story in detail, and then look for other symbols of God's love — in John's Gospel and in more familiar surroundings.

Way in

Light a candle at the beginning of the session, or as you start to read through and reflect on today's notes. Place it on a table or a shelf where there is room for other objects to be put near it without danger. Take time from your reading to look at it, the shape of the flame, its colours, the way it burns in stillness and moves with the air around. Be attentive to it.

Amazing grace

Read John 9. Read the whole chapter at once, as a complete story. If there are several of you, listen to one person reading it, or a small group who take the voices of different characters. Follow the reading with a period of silence.

Then sing together John Newton's hymn, 'Amazing grace...'

Keynote reading
John 9.1–41

Light a candle:
it burns in
stillness and
moves with the
air around

Reflect

How do the people in the story understand what Jesus is doing in the life of this man:

—the disciples?

—the man himself?

—the neighbours and onlookers?

—the Pharisees?

—the man's parents?

As a group, or as individuals, write down a few words that sum up the attitude of each person or group.

Symbols

In this story, sight becomes a symbol of our awareness of God.

Think of some other symbols for God, and our relationship with God, that can be found in St John's Gospel (*e.g. 2.10; 3.3; 3.8; 4.14; 6.35; 8.12; 10.14; 12.24; 13.12–17; 15.1–5...*).

Let the group — without too much talking — walk around the room and find something that for them is a picture of their relationship with God, e.g. spectacles which help you to see clearly; a seashell which enfolds and protects the creature inside; a piece of bread which nourishes; a glass of water...

Place each object carefully by the candle.

Sit in silence watching the candle for a little while.

PRAYER

Thank God, in your own words, and/or sing one verse of 'Amazing grace...'

Study 3 *Holding on and letting go*

AIM

To explore the story of Lazarus and learn from it how to face the death of those we know and love and how we approach it ourselves.

Preparation for the whole group

This week's study is based on one extended Gospel story: John

Sight becomes a symbol of our awareness of God

Keynote readings
John 11.1–57
John 12.1–26

11.1 to 12.26. Members of the group might like to read it through in their own time. Much of the session will be taken in reading it again, reflectively, and with time for discussion. The questions below are also ones that readers can ask themselves individually.

You will need 10 small stones, or 10 gloves.

Way in

Place a cross or a candle in a prominent place. Lighting the candle, pray:

God, who said, 'Let there be light',

forgive us that we choose to walk in the dark;

as we see your love in the clear light of Jesus,

help us to become children of the light. Amen

Read in stages the story of the death of Lazarus. After each stage, and when the question has been discussed, put a stone, or a glove (like a hand) by the cross or candle — to represent the people named.

John 11.1–16 **The doubts of the disciples**

● How do I (we) respond to crisis? What would we have done in this situation?

John 11.17–27 **The faith of Martha**

● If you were writing a card to someone recently bereaved, what would you say in it? Would you feel able to share your faith?

John 11.28–37 **The tears of Mary**

● Why do you think Jesus wept? What emotions do people see in Jesus *(verses 33 and 36)*? Does this surprise you?

What emotions do people see in Jesus?

John 11.38–44 **The loosing of Lazarus**

● How can the graveside be a place where we glimpse God's glory?

John 11.45–57 **The challenge to the onlookers**

● If you had been an onlooker, expecting to see Jesus in Jerusalem, what would you have expected him to do?

John 12.12–19 **The hope of the pilgrims**

● Describe a time when you have been part of a large crowd, sharing a celebration, for instance. How was hope shown?

When have you done a foolish thing because you felt that was where your faith was leading you?

Keynote reading
John 14.1–14

Esther John

John 12.20-26 **The curiosity of the Gentiles**
● When have you had to let go of something you cherished? When have you done a foolish thing because you felt that was where your faith was leading you?

PRAYER

God of wisdom
thank you for those with courage to ask questions.
God of surprises,
thank you that out of loss comes new life. Amen

Study 4 *Walking in the light*

AIM

To reflect on the lives of two contemporary martyrs in the light of John 14.1–14.

Way in
Sing together, 'Jesus the Lord said, "I am the way..."' and then read John 14.5–6 and reflect on these verses in silence.

Preparation
You will need to photocopy each of the mini-biographies printed below.

Two contemporary stories
Divide the group into two, perhaps men and women if numbers permit, each to read one of the mini-biographies you have copied. Ask someone in each group to read the story aloud.

Esther John was born in Qamar Zia in 1929 in India, into a large family which, after the partition of India, moved to Pakistan. She was well educated, first in a government school, then in a Christian one, where, influenced by the faith of a teacher, she read Isaiah 53 and was converted.

In Karachi, she met a missionary, Marian Laugesan, who gave her a copy of the New Testament. She read it secretly and her Christian faith grew. After seven years, she ran away from home, to avoid an arranged marriage with a Muslim husband. She worked in an orphanage in Karachi, taking the Christian name Esther John.

Her family urged her to remain and marry, but instead she

went north to the Punjab in 1955, worked in a mission hospital and then trained in the United Bible Training Centre as an evangelist. Then she travelled among the villages, working alongside women in the fields, teaching them to read and preaching the gospel.
Esther kept in touch with her family, but there was often tension. In February 1960 she was murdered in her bed. No one knew who had done it, but all believed it was because she was a Christian.

Janani Luwum was a young school teacher in Uganda when, during a charismatic revival, he was converted to Christianity in 1948. He started to try to change other lives, preaching against alcohol and tobacco, and was criticized for disturbing the peace. He trained as a catechist and then for ordination. By 1956 he was a priest, then he became principal of the college where he studied, and in 1969 Bishop of Northern Uganda. In those 20 years he made his name as a visionary, energetic and committed leader — not afraid of controversy.

Janani Luwum

Idi Amin, head of the Ugandan Army, overthrew the elected government of Uganda and quickly became a corrupt and despotic ruler. There was discrimination and persecution of many, including Luwum's own Acoli people. In 1974 Janani Luwum was elected archbishop. While working hard to reform the church, challenging Christians not to conform to 'the powers of darkness', he pleaded with those in power for those who were being persecuted. With other Christian and Muslim leaders he addressed the political issues. In 1976, after they had delivered a strong protest against government violence, the Church leaders were all summoned to Kampala, where Luwum was singled out and kept back when the others had left. He was taken away and murdered, but his body has never been found.

Bring the two groups together and let each in turn share in telling from memory the stories of Esther John and Janani Luwum.
● What do these very different people, from different continents, have in common?
Read John 14.1–14.

● Which verse seems to you to relate most strongly to this session?

● What other people do you know about, whose courage and lives put them alongside those whose stories you have just read?

PRAYER

Close with extempore prayer.

Week 5 *'Live in me'*

Keynote reading
John 15.1–10

AIM

To reflect, in the light of our own experiences, on Jesus 'the vine'.

Begin with this meditation:

The Vine

Close your eyes and imagine you are a plant.
Not any plant, a particular kind:
a climbing, clinging plant grown against a wall,
the sunny wall of a house in a hot country;
but it is a country where you are at home,
and you grow well.
You have been planted here
by the owner of the house because you will grow well
and because you will give welcome shade.
So a trellis has been built —
a framework of weathered wood —

'Feel your roots seeking water deep down, drawing nourishment into your whole being'

Jan S Pickard,
Dandelions and
Thistles

and you have sent out your tendrils onto the trellis,
taken hold and are growing there, too,
your luxuriant leaves shading the terrace underneath,
and the benches where people can sit
in the heat of the day.

You have been here a long time.
Your main stem is old and gnarled,
rough to the touch but beautiful in its own way.
Your roots are deep.
Feel them going down into the earth,
unseen, but still as much part of you
as the leaves that dance in the breeze.
Feel your roots seeking water deep down,
drawing nourishment into your whole being.

Feel your leaves draw energy from the sun
and turn it, in their cells, into strength
for the whole of you.
Feel your tendrils alive,
sensitively seeking new directions
in which you can grow,
and holding on to rough stone and warm wood
so that the wind does not damage you.
Feel your fruits forming, filling out,
becoming juicy, delicious, nourishing.
Feel how each part of you is connected
and draws strength from the other parts.
Feel joy in being the healthy fruitful plant
that God made you to be.

People are coming down the track,
a group of people talking.
They come to the house, stop on the terrace.
Someone from the house brings them cool drinks.
They sit in your shade, talking.
Mostly they are listening to one man,
who seems to be explaining something to them.
They look puzzled.
Suddenly he reaches out, touches your stem,
gestures to your leaves and fruit, and says,
'I am the vine'.   *Jan S Pickard*
                               Dandelions and Thistles
                               (Wild Goose Publications)

In what ways do you think Jesus expects us today to be fruitful?

Read John 15.1–10.

● In what ways do you think Jesus expects us today to be fruitful?
● How can we become more fruitful?
● Is there a difference between unity and uniformity?
● How can relationships be strengthened with Christ,
  with fellow Christians and within the community?

PRAYER

Christ, True Vine, may our lives become more connected,
to each other, but most of all to you.
May we draw strength from the life that flows from you;
may we go on growing in faith, all our lives long;
may we bear fruit for the good of all. Amen

Study 6 *Through the darkness*

Keynote readings
John 17.20–23
John 18.1–40
John 19.1–42

AIM

To reflect on the Passion story of Jesus and, by recognizing our own failures mirrored in it, to find hope and make our own new beginnings.

Being prayed for
Begin by thinking or talking about the experience of being prayed for. When have you known that others have been praying for you? How did it help?

Follow this with a time of silent prayer, for each other and for the world.

The Passion of our Lord
Read aloud John 17.20-23.

After this prayer in the Upper Room, Jesus went with his disciples to Gethsemane. There, while he was praying, he was arrested.

Much of this session could be spent on reading — in short sections — chapters 18 and 19 of John, listening to music, or singing, praying or simply reflecting silently after each reading.

Notice the contrast between Jesus and Peter *(John 18.1–18)*. Look at Jesus' calm courage, shown in verses 4, 8 and 11. In contrast look at Peter's confusion of mind. 'In trying to defend Jesus, Peter used the wrong weapon, had the wrong motive, acted under the wrong orders and accomplished the wrong result.' Do you agree?

Jesus is bound but free in a deeper way

Again, look at Peter in the second half of this chapter, free but trapped by his own lies. Jesus is bound *(verses 12,13, 24)*, but free in a deeper way *(verses 20 and 23)*.

Then look at the contrast between Jesus and Pilate. Though in authority, Pilate is unsure, afraid, in many ways powerless *(verses 8, 10, 12, 13, and 16)*. He tries different approaches *(18.31 and 39; 19,1–3 and 15)*. Jesus shows a different kind of authority in both words and silence *(19.9 and 11)*.

Reflect on this in silence.

In general, compared to the women who followed Jesus on his last journey, stood faithfully at the foot of the cross, and watched at the tomb, men — both disciples and Jesus' accusers — do not come out of the Passion story well.

There were, however, 'the disciple whom Jesus loved' and two other men, members of the Jewish Council: Joseph of Arimathaea and Nicodemus. Look at their parts in the story: John 19.38–42.

Imagine this theme and pray:

In the secrecy of our hearts, there is hope.
We cannot always find the words, or the courage,
to proclaim what we believe.
But, as Nicodemus and Joseph found,
there are still things that we can do for you —
our God, who lived and died to make us whole.
We can take your broken body, hold it in our minds,
care for it, anoint it with our tears;
we can find a space in our full lives
to remember and reflect on your death,
and to watch with those few who remained faithful,
and did what needed to be done.
Help us to learn patience, from them, and the women.
For in the silence of the grave there is also hope.
Amen

In the silence of the grave there is also hope

39

EASTER — RESURRECTION

Study 1 *The victory of love*

Key readings
John 20.1–18
Luke 24.13–49
1 John 1.1 to 2.1

AIM

To consider what is involved in effective witnessing to the risen Christ, particularly in the context of the corporate testimony of local churches.

Warm-up

As a group, see if anyone can resolve the following problem, using the rules indicated.

Using four straight lines only and not taking the pen off the paper, cover all nine dots in the pattern below without retracing any part of the lines already drawn.

```
        *       *       *


        *       *       *


        *       *       *
```

(Solution on page 124)

If you didn't solve the problem, reflect where you went wrong: most likely you began from your own presuppositions — namely that you needed to stay within the boundaries of the nine dots themselves.

Discuss: how often are problems solved when you go beyond accepted boundaries — presupposed or laid down?

How often are problems solved when you go beyond accepted boundaries — presupposed or laid down?

Mary's testimony

'For Mary, a key figure in the appearance stories, Resurrection was not the first thing that came to mind, even with the pile-up of indications that something had happened.

'If we are always controlled by presuppositions and

close our minds to insights and indicators that there might be more in it than we think, we rob ourselves of the opportunity to be surprised by joy. We learn from Mary's experience that knowing the risen Lord is a gift of his own self-revelation... It is a matter of being lovingly affirmed and having renewed and joyful knowledge of the presence of the living Lord...'

Burchel Taylor, Words for Today 2000 *(IBRA)*

When have you been hampered from seeing the truth of a situation because of presuppositions? Share such moments with the group if you feel able.

TESTIMONY and WITNESS...

● What are your presuppositions about these words? Are they coloured by your past experience of testimonies? Are they the domain of individuals only?

● Are they words you are comfortable with?

Read 1 John 1.1–2.2 and the following comment:

'The life-transforming experience, which results from an encounter and response in faith to the living Christ, is both the basis and the inspiration of faithful Christian testimony. This testimony is not an option but an essential expression of the transformed life...

Christian testimony is backed by first-hand experience of the living Lord Jesus Christ who is none other than the same Jesus, the Word that became flesh and dwelt in our midst. The conviction and earnestness of personal testimony are certainly significant. Yet the testimony is also the expression of a corporate experience which adds to its power and effectiveness. The writer speaks not as an isolated individual with a private and exclusive experience, but as a member of a community with shared first-hand experience of Christ and shared commitment to make it known to others. The aim is also to widen the embrace of the fellowship through the testimony. Isn't this a serious challenge to the rugged individualism and self-centredness of our times, not unknown in Christian circles?

Christian testimony is not only of words but also of a transparent life. This is a life of fidelity and honesty.

When have you been hampered from seeing the truth of a situation because of presuppositions?

This life is assured of the renewing grace of forgiveness and benefits from interceding advocacy by the One most worthy of all, the living exalted Lord. Living with this knowledge gives our testimony integrity, trustworthiness, confidence and humility.'

Burchel Taylor, Words for Today 2000 *(IBRA)*

● How do you react to this description of true testimony?

● Is this a fair assessment?

● If so, what impact does the assertion of corporate witness have on you and your local church?

The objective of our testimony should be the disclosure of the risen Christ

● The objective of our testimony should be the disclosure of the risen Christ as we, as a church, enflesh the Word again in our community life. If we have known an experience of the risen Christ, do we feel released for worship and witness, fellowship and discipleship?

The practical out-working

What are the implications of our understanding of true testimony in terms of effective witness

● for our pattern of Sunday and our life together in fellowship?

● for our building-based activities?

● for our dealings with the local community?

● for our dealings with other churches in our locality?

ACTION

Plan to do one thing together which will be an effective witness within the local community.

PRAYER

Let every member of the group offer a testimony — in one or two sentences — of how they find strength for living.

Offer up your total witness in thanksgiving to God.

Study 2 *Community of love*

AIM

To explore the key sentiments of Christian community — a sense of significance as individuals and a sense of solidarity as members of one another.

Key readings
John 21.1–25
1 John 4.7–21

Way in

In twos or threes, make lists of the characteristics of the 'Ideal Christian Community'.

Come together as a group and try to place the characteristics in order of priority.

Genuine community

David Clarke, who has spent many years writing on the nature of community, suggests that although we can define community as a gathering of people with common interests and ideals, the acid test of genuine community is in being able to enter a community and detect an awareness of significance within each member as well as a sense of solidarity or belonging to the community itself.

● Reflect on your own church community. What is it that gives you a sense of significance or not? Does it depend only on taking responsibility and thereby earning status, or on the way people treat you?

● How does the way Jesus treated people compare with your conclusions?

● What makes you feel that you belong to your church community?

What makes you feel that you belong to your church community?

Biblical reflection

Read 1 John 4.7–21. Is this the core of Christian love and therefore of Christian community?

'...We reach the core of Christian love: "We love because he first loved us" *(verse 19)*. It is God's love which gives us the confidence and sense of self-worth to reach out to others in love. It is our confidence in God's love which enables us to put aside our fear of rejection and offer his love to others. It is God's unshakeable love for us which makes us love and value ourselves.

Is the test of true Christian community whether it demonstrates the life of the Triune God: Many in One and One in Many?

The proof of God's love for us is that he sent his Son to free us from the prison of sin and draw us into the life of the Trinity.'

Kate Hughes, Words for Today 2000 *(IBRA)*

Is the test of true Christian community whether it demonstrates the life of the Triune God: Many in One and One in Many?

ACTION

What can you do to help your local church to become a community of love? Decide on ONE practical thing which you could do, as a group or an individual, to show love for your brothers and sisters in Christ.

PRAYER

Read together or sing and reflect on the song 'Turning the World Upside Down'.

Thank you, Lord, for helping us to find our significance in your self-giving for each of us.

Help us to lose ourselves in making others feel their worth.

May our sense of solidarity as the Body of Christ enable others to identify with you in the fellowship of God's people.

Study 3 *People of faith*

Key readings
Acts 3.1–19
Acts 4.1–31
1 Peter 1.13–25

AIM

To recognize that we are part of the ongoing story of God and people of faith.

Way in

In her book *Never Mind The Gap* (NCEC, 1999), Joan King suggests that one of the roles grandparents play is that of 'Living Ancestors'. She suggests that they can communicate family history to grandchildren, creating a link with the past and helping them to feel secure with roots in both the past and the present.

Share in small groups some of the stories of your family which have been passed on to you by 'Living Ancestors'.

From one generation to another

Look at the key readings for this study and notice where past and present are woven together. Where do you see the inspiration for the future?

● What makes you who you are?

● Imagine you are a grandparent. What stories about yourself would you share with a grandchild?

What is the value of sharing our stories?

Discuss some of the statements listed below in the context of your own church and locality:

● Telling our stories puts us in the picture. It gives depth to our knowledge of those who 'sit in the pews'.

● No longer strangers. Refugees need to share their stories. Apply this to your local community, especially newcomers.

● Helps us to understand where we belong — our power base!

Do you know the stories of your church and how it came to be in your town?

Lives of the Saints – the next episode! That's us...

ACTION

Encourage people in your church to share their stories. Create an informal opportunity for this to happen.

PRAYER

Give thanks for the saints you know, and end by offering the Grace to each other as the people of faith.

Telling our stories puts us in the picture. It gives depth to our knowledge of those who 'sit in the pews'

Lives of the Saints – the next episode! That's us...

LIVING ENCOUNTERS

Study 1 *Encounter with Judaism*

Keynote readings

Genesis 17.1–21
Leviticus 11.1–12,
41–45
Leviticus 19.1–4, 9–18,
32–37
Deuteronomy 6.1–9
Psalm 23

What difference would it make to the life of your home to have the words of Deuteronomy 9.4–9 affixed to your doorpost?

AIM

To develop and deepen our understanding of Judaism as a living faith.

Way in

Every Jewish home has a *mezuzah* fixed to its doorpost. This is a small box which contains a tiny scroll bearing the words of Deuteronomy 9.4–9. Read these verses together. What difference would it make to the life of your home to have these words affixed to your doorpost?

'Israel is instructed to focus on the Divine Oneness that transcends all human thought. In such engagement she discovers that the love of God is an all-consuming passion that embraces every aspect of our being.

The ultimate task of the Jew is to bring this sense of God into the everyday world, by teaching and understanding the words of the tradition, and applying them in all the situations of life. Such teaching is the first and most vital responsibility of parents to their children.

We are physical as well as intellectual beings; in binding the words of the Torah in phylacteries upon our hands and forehead, we recall the inner task of bringing our most physical desires into the realm of the holy and seek to restore our minds to the tasks of study and devotion.'

Jonathan Gorsky, Words for Today 2000 (*IBRA*)

Reflect together on what we can learn from this tradition.

The Covenant

Read Genesis 17.1–21.

'The Covenant relationship, a kind of marriage, with God is the basis of Jewish life, and circumcision is one of the rituals which have distinguished the Jewish community and held it together.

'As marriage implies infinitely more than the basic agreement between husband and wife, so covenant is the beginning of a relationship that transcends its legal origin. It becomes a profound personal engagement that survives even the blatant dereliction of its basic terms, for it is rooted in the love of God and His people Israel which endures for all eternity.'

Jonathan Gorsky, Words for Today 2000 *(IBRA)*

● What can the rest of the world learn from this Jewish tradition to strengthen their communities?

● What can Christians learn from Israel's Covenant relationship to God to enrich our life as the Body of Christ?

The Sabbath

The Jewish *Shabbat* begins with a meal at sunset on Friday evening. The family comes together to relax at the end of the working week, but the meal is full of meaning:

'...Two loaves, reminiscent of the double portion of biblical manna, are placed on the table with a bottle of wine and a goblet. The loaves are covered by a second cloth and candlesticks complete the setting. Candles are lit, usually by the woman of the house, just before the onset of the Sabbath. Candle-lighting is accompanied by a brief blessing and sometimes a quiet personal prayer.

Before the meal the family sanctify the Sabbath day verbally and everyone has a little wine, followed by the breaking of bread. The meal is a relaxed occasion and, in a traditional household, Sabbath songs are sung between courses.

For the whole of the Sabbath, orthodox Jews do no creative work. Cars, televisions, telephones and fax machines are forgotten for 25 hours of tranquillity. All cooking is done in advance and food left on a covered stove for the three meals that are taken on Friday night and the following day.

On *Shabbat* — the Sabbath — the world is seen as it was

What can Christians learn from Israel's Covenant relationship to God to enrich our life as the Body of Christ?

47

What can Christians learn from the spirit of the Sabbath?

at the beginning of time, and it becomes a place of holiness, as at the first Sabbath, the seventh day of creation. The Sabbath is a moment of intimacy between God and Israel, a sign for ever of the Divine presence in this world, and a time when we realize that the sanctification of life is the ultimate purpose of all existence.'

Jonathan Gorsky, Words for Today 2000 *(IBRA)*

● What can Christians learn from the spirit of the Sabbath?

The dietary laws

Equal care is taken over the preparation of food. In Leviticus 11 certain meats are forbidden. Birds, animals and fish are part of God's creation, and human beings may not exploit them to satisfy their desire. They are to be used responsibly. Other texts stress the importance of humane slaughter. All meat must be *Kosher*.

● How can we develop a greater reverence for the living world?

The Lord is my Shepherd

Read Psalm 23. Reflect together on this psalm as a treasure we hold in common with the Jewish community. Why has this become a best-loved psalm frequently turned to by people who do not attend church?

PRAYER

Give thanks for all the rich traditions we have received from Judaism.

Pray that we may grow in our reverence of the Scriptures and in strength and grace to put them into practice.

Study 2 *Celebration and suffering*

Keynote readings
Deuteronomy 16.1–17
Psalm 22
Isaiah 2.1–5

AIM

To enact the main features of the Passover meal and reflect on its meaning.

Preparation

You will need a small table that can be seen by everyone. Place on it the following items:

48

—*two candles;*
—*a dish of salt water;*
—*some* Matzos — *unleavened bread (available in most supermarkets);*
—*a glass of wine (or non-alcoholic equivalent);*
—*a large plate containing some parsley (one sprig per person);*
—*a small dish of horseradish* — maror — *bitter herbs;*
—Charoseth — *a sweet paste* — *made from equal quantities of grated apples and ground almonds with a little cinnamon and wine (just a small amount for everyone to taste);*
—*a roast egg;*
—*a shankbone of lamb.*
Make photocopies of the abridged liturgy for the Passover meal.

The Passover meal
The words printed in bold type are to be said by all.

The leader lights the candles:

May the festival lights we now kindle

Inspire us to use our powers

To heal and not to harm,

To help and not to hinder,

To bless and not to curse,

To serve you, O God of freedom.

The leader then holds up the cup, saying:

Blessed are you, Lord God, King of the universe, Creator of the fruit of the vine.

Blessed are you, Lord God, King of the universe. You have chosen us from among all people; you have given us joy and gladness, and brought us to this celebration of our freedom.

The cup is passed around for everyone to drink.

The leader then takes the karpas *(parsley), dips it in salt and distributes it, saying:*

Blessed are you, Lord our God. You have given us special days for joy ... the feast of our freedom.

Similarly, the Matzos *(unleavened bread) is shared, and the leader says:*

This is the bread of suffering which our fathers ate in the

land of Egypt.

Let everyone who is hungry come in and eat. All who are in need, let them come and celebrate the Passover.

The youngest child then asks:

Why is this night different from all other nights?

Why is this night different from all other nights?

Leader:

Our parents went down into Egypt, but the Egyptians treated us harshly and made us their slaves. We cried unto the Lord and he heard us. With a mighty and outstretched arm, God brought us out of Egypt, with great signs and wonders. Blessed is God who keeps his promise to Israel.

Youngest child:

Why do we eat lamb on this night?

Leader:

It is to remind us of the death of the first-born of the Egyptians. God commanded our forefathers to roast a lamb for their meal and sprinkle their doorposts with its blood. The first-born in these homes were spared. This lamb was an offering made to God who led them out of slavery.

Youngest child:

Why do we eat unleavened bread on this night?

Leader:

It is in memory of the flight of our forebears from Egypt when there was no time for the dough to become leavened.

Youngest child:

Why do we drink wine on this night?

Leader:

Wine was drunk by our forebears to celebrate their deliverance from Egypt.

Youngest child:

Why do we eat bitter herbs?

Leader:

When our parents were slaves in Egypt, the Egyptians made their lives bitter with hard labour and oppression and caused them to shed many bitter tears.

The leader may then briefly and entertainingly tell the story of the ten plagues and deliverance from Egypt.

Let us praise and thank God who took us out of slavery into freedom, out of suffering into gladness, out of mourning into this celebration, out of darkness into light...

This is a very abridged version (extracted from *Celebrating One World*, CAFOD) of what goes on. The asking of the four questions by the youngest child is the introduction to a lot of story-telling, which happens in a very enjoyable way. Many psalms are sung, and the meal (stewed or roast lamb) is enjoyed together. The *charoseth* (sweet paste) symbolizes the mortar with which the Hebrews made bricks.

An empty chair and glass of wine are left for the spirit of Elijah, and at some point in the meal, a child is asked to open the door and let him in.

And four cups of wine are shared with further prayers in the full liturgy.

Reflection

● How is our understanding of redemption helped by Jewish experience and thought?

● Jews treasure this custom of retelling the story of the Exodus. How important a place have we given to story-telling in our traditions? What can we learn here from the Jews?

Biblical reflection
From the time of their slavery in Egypt to the present day, the Jewish people have suffered much throughout their history. Imagine you are a Jew with memories of relatives who died in the Holocaust, and read Psalm 22.

Allow a time of silence, and then share together the feelings and insights which come out of this experience.

● What do we learn from the psalmist's honesty about the sense of isolation he experienced in his suffering? How does he move from basic human feelings to a deeper awareness of God's presence?

How is our understanding of redemption helped by Jewish experience and thought?

Read the following comment from Jonathan Gorsky and reflect together:

'If faith is based on Divine intervention and, when we are in dire need, no help is forthcoming, then our grounds for believing are shattered beyond repair. But the source of the Psalmist's fidelity lies elsewhere. His first thought is the transcendent holiness that he encounters in the life of prayer, and he then recalls the miraculous wonder that accompanies the birth of children. Such signs of the Divine cannot be quenched even by overwhelming evil and, in their presence, we cannot conceive of a wholly meaningless universe. The sense of God is continual and intimate, and it is, paradoxically, the ground of the Psalmist's anguish. It is not the Divine absence, but the constancy of God's presence, that makes him confront the mystery of suffering.'

Jonathan Gorsky, Words for Today 2000 *(IBRA)*

What are the 'touching points' between Judaism and Christianity?

● From our brief exploration of Judaism in the last two studies, what are the 'touching points' between Judaism and Christianity?

PRAYER

Pray for a deeper understanding of the faith of the Jewish community; and that we may learn from their faithfulness to God through long periods of exile, dispersion and suffering.

ACTION

Try to arrange for your group to visit a local synagogue, or invite a member of the Jewish community to come to your group and answer questions.

Study 3 *Encounters with other faiths*

Keynote readings
Acts 10.1–48
Genesis 1.26–31
Psalm 104.24–30

AIM

To discover more about the oneness of all humanity, and to develop a greater understanding of people of other faiths.

Way in

Give each member of the group a copy of the following quotations, and ask them to write by the side of each the name of the world religion from which the saying comes:

1. 'Hear, O Israel, the Lord is our God, one Lord, and you must love the Lord your God with all your heart and mind and soul and strength.'

2. 'He alone is pure whose heart is pure.'

3. 'Anger must be overcome by the absence of anger;
   Evil must be overcome by good;
   Greed must be overcome by liberality;
   Lies must be overcome by truth.'

4. 'You must not retaliate when another does you injury.'

5. 'In the city joyful dwell all the saints of God. Neither suffering nor sorrow is found there.'

6. 'He will not enter hell, who has faith equal to a grain of mustard seed in his heart.'

7. 'You shall not seek revenge, or cherish anger towards your kinsfolk; you shall love your neighbour as a man like yourself. I am the Lord.'

8. 'Thou who stealest the hearts of those that love thee, drown me in the sea of Thy love.'

9. 'The Divine Mercy is perfect, in the sense that it answers every need. It is universal in the sense that it spreads alike over those who merit it and those who do not merit it.'

10. 'From the unreal lead me to the real;
    From darkness lead me to light;
    From death lead me to immortality.'

11. 'If someone has done you wrong, do not repay him with a wrong.'

12. 'He who gladly accepts the suffering of this world brings salvation to the world.'

The answers are given on pages 124 and 125.

● Were you surprised by any of the answers? Share your impressions.

● What do the sayings tell us about the way God is revealed through other major world faiths?

Hinduism

Buddhism

Sikhism

Islam

Christianity

● What experience does the group have of encounter with people of other faiths? Impressions from visits to other parts of the world? Or from more close encounter if you live in a multi-faith community?

● Read Genesis 1.26–31. These verses remind us that all humankind is made in God's image, so is it really surprising when we discover what is 'holy' in other religions?

Crossing bridges
Read Acts 10.1–16.

In the last study, we looked at Jewish dietary laws. Imagine Peter's reaction to the command in his dream to eat what he had been brought up to abhor. The dream was a backcloth to an encounter that would take place between Peter and Cornelius, a Roman who was interested in learning more about Judaism. For Peter, such an encounter meant entering new territory and, from the standpoint of his religious loyalties, raised questions about compromising his faith.

To what extent does the religion we cherish inhibit us from hearing what the Holy Spirit is challenging us to do today?

● To what extent does the religion we cherish inhibit us from hearing what the Holy Spirit is challenging us to do today?

● What aspects of our religion, or attitudes, hold us back?
Read Acts 10.17–33.

'Changes in theological understanding are often preceded by changes in experience. Christians who make friends with people of other faiths usually discover that their friends are filled with deep faith, sincere commitment and high moral sensitivity. The result is that condemnatory generalizations about other faiths cease to make sense.'

Elizabeth Harris, Words for Today 2000 *(IBRA)*

Reflect together on this statement.

Read Acts 10.34–43.

● What challenge does verse 34 make to us in a multi-faith society?

NB Even if you do not live in a multi-faith society, what you think about this issue matters. Younger people who move away to study or work carry with them the attitudes they have heard expressed at home, at church and in the community.

Learning from others

So often Christians who live among people of other religions discover an integrity and depth of faith that puts theirs to shame. A Christian told me how sometimes, when phoning her Hindu or Muslim friends, the response is, 'Sorry, we're at prayer at the moment. Can we ring you back?' That never happens, she said, when I ring a Christian home!

Reflect again on what can be learnt from the sayings from other faiths on page 53.

PRAYER

Creator, Parent God,
who gave birth to all that exists,
you look with pride upon the potential and goodness
of all you created and continue to love it all.
Give us your perfect love that crosses barriers,
and when you lead us into dialogue and debates
where our knowledge is pitifully inadequate,
let us not shrink from the challenge,
but make us sensitive to the spirit of honest inquiry
and help us to bear the pain of our own vulnerability.

ACTION

Explore the possibilities of inviting a person of another faith to come and share with you what his or her faith means, or arrange a visit to a place of worship.

Study 4 *A new respect*

AIM

To look more closely at some of the 'touching points' of the major faiths.

Way in

Read Mark 7.24–30. If Jesus was here today, and the

Keynote readings
Ruth 1.1–22
Jonah 4.1–11
Mark 7.24–30
Mark 9.38–41
Mark 12.28–34
Acts 17.16–28

woman was a Hindu, what would be his response?

Reverence

Elizabeth Harris spent seven years in Sri Lanka living among Buddhists to learn from them. She tells how she found true devotion, a people of real faith, full of love and compassion, and full of a spiritual sense; they taught her to think more deeply about prayer and to value silence. 'And so I was forced to ask the question', she says, 'Is this blessed by God? If I believe in a God of love, I must believe it is blessed. For wherever there is compassion and spiritual awareness, there is God.' In all the time she spent with them in their temples, in meditation, listening to chants, lighting candles, she did not feel she was betraying her Christian faith, but showing reverence for a great teacher and experiencing bonds of love with Buddhists there.

She discovered many 'touching points' but her experience also confirmed that it is not possible to iron out all the differences and to find a common core. We need to respect those differences.

It is arrogance for Christians to believe that only they have the truth

She maintains that it is arrogance for Christians to believe that only they have the truth. This attitude denies that God is at work in all the world. All religions are unique in their own way. She saw her seven years of learning from the people and texts of Buddhism as 'a bridge' between people who know very little of one another. Her role was to build trust and understanding.

Reflect together on this experience and then read Matthew 28.19: 'Go therefore and make disciples of all nations...' Focus on the word 'disciple'. The Greek word, *mathetes*, means 'one who learns'; the text does not indicate the need for conversion as we have often been conditioned into thinking.

● How is the Holy Spirit leading us to interpret this text today?

Love and peace

Read Mark 12.28–34. Jesus' answer is not a new one, but affirms two fundamental aspects of Judaism and most other faiths — love of God and love for others.

- Make a list of other ways in which Jesus showed respect for Judaism, e.g. 'I came not to destroy the Law or the prophets...' What might he have said if he had been born in a Buddhist, Hindu or Islamic community?
- At the heart of all major faiths there is also a deep desire for peace, within both the individual and the world. It is essential for world peace that we explore more ways of working together for the benefit of all. How can you begin to do this where you live?

We are to build friendships out of love and for their own sake — as bridges of understanding. In God's time, not ours, the Spirit of God will do whatever converting may be necessary and that may need to happen as much within ourselves as in others!

At the heart of all major faiths there is a deep desire for peace, within both the individual and the world

PRAYER

Reflect together on the meaning and spirituality of the following prayers from different faiths. Then use them as your closing prayers:

God is greater. Glory be to Thee, O God, and praise. Blessed is Thy Name and transcendent Thy majesty. There is no god but Thee.

I turn my face to Him who gave being to the heavens and the earth in true devotion. Not for me the fellowship of false worship. Truly my worship and my oblation, my living and my dying, are God's alone, the Lord of all being. For there is no god beside Him.

From Salat *(Islam)*

My prayer to You is through the hiddenness of Your gentleness, the gentleness of Your way of dealing, through the very beauty of Your elusiveness, through the greatness of Your might and the utter secret of Your power, by all that is untold in Your transcendence.

From Ahmad al-Tijani *(Islam)*

Thou my mother, and my father thou.
Thou my friend, and my teacher thou.
Thou my wisdom, and my riches thou.
Thou art all to me, O God of all gods.

From the Ramanuja *(Hinduism)*

'Teach us love, compassion, and honour That we may heal the earth And heal each other.'

Ojibway people of Canada

Grandfather,
Look at our brokenness.
We know that in all creation
Only the human family
Has strayed from the Sacred Way.
We know that we are the ones
Who are divided
And we are the ones
Who must come back together
To walk in the Sacred Way.
Grandfather,
Sacred One,
Teach us love, compassion, and honour
That we may heal the earth
And heal each other.

Ojibway people of Canada

ACTION

If you do not know much about other faiths, then make sure you read some books about them. Or, better still, get to know a person of another faith.

THE SPIRIT IN THE WORLD

NOTES
BY
MAUREEN
EDWARDS

Study 1 *Making us one*

AIM

To recognize the movement of the Spirit among the Christian community in the Holy Land and in our own neighbourhood 2000 years after the first Pentecost.

Way in

● Have any members of the group visited the Holy Land? Draw on their experience and encourage them to share impressions.

● What is the current social/political situation in the Holy Land?

● What do you know of the Church there at the present time?

Try to imagine you were one of the waiting community of the followers of Jesus and read together Acts 2.1–21. Share any insights which come from this reading.

The 'living stones'

Today there are about 114,000 Christians in Israel proper and another 51,000 in occupied territories. That is a significant Christian presence: 2.4% of the population. A diversity and richness of traditions are to be seen in the 13 main denominations, including the Greek Catholic (Melkite) Church, the Roman Catholic Church, the Orthodox Churches (Armenian, Syrian, Ethiopian, Greek, Coptic, Russian, and Romanian), Anglicans and Lutherans. These diverse Churches relate to one another through the Middle East Council of Churches in Jerusalem.

Of special interest are the Orthodox Churches, which are distinctively different with their use of icons, incense, ceremony, bright colours and ornate buildings. The absence of pews gives a sense of informality. People come

Keynote readings
Acts 2.1–21
Ephesians 2.11–22
Ephesians 3.1–21
Ephesians 4.1–16
Romans 8.22–27

and go freely, sometimes only to light a candle and say a prayer. Services can last for up to four hours; time doesn't matter. The strange music and biblical liturgy, although not understood by most visitors, create an atmosphere for reflection and meditation.

The Armenian Orthodox churches mostly have little adornment, but their priests can be seen in distinctive black hoods, which are designed to make them look like walking churches, i.e. a church walking in the world.

● What might we learn from this tradition to enrich our spiritual journey?

An inclusive faith
Read Ephesians 3.1–13.

'Paul, in his letter to the Ephesians, reminds us that the gospel enables people of all nationalities and cultures to share with the Jews in God's blessings. He adds that they are members of the same body and share in the promise that God made through Christ Jesus. Yet, given the political divisions and human frailties in this land of the Resurrection, those of faith — Christians and non-Christians alike — do not always recognize how to be inclusive, or how to think of their neighbour as a fellow human being created in the likeness and image of God.'

Harry Hagopian, Words for Today 2000 *(IBRA)*

● How typical is this statement of the relationships between churches in your area?

In what ways are the churches in your area sharing the love of Christ?

● In what ways are the churches in your area sharing the love of Christ?

● What examples are there of working and witnessing together?

One body
Continue thinking about your local churches.

● What value do the differences in architecture and the ways you worship have for you?

● What prevents you from achieving closer unity?

Read Ephesians 4.1–16. Ask members of the group to select a phrase from this reading and to say why it challenges them.

- Do we really recognize the ecumenical movement as the work of the Spirit?
- What do we understand by the word 'church'?

PRAYER

Pray for the peoples of the Holy Land, for peace with justice;

for the Churches there and the ecumenical fellowship centred on the Middle East Council of Churches in Jerusalem;

that the Holy Spirit may draw together all our Churches and enable us to learn from and to be enriched by one another's faith and experience.

ACTION

- When visiting the Holy Land, make a special effort to meet with some of the local Christians — rather than simply visiting sites of religious or historic interest. Attend Sunday worship in a local church, and get to know a Palestinian congregation.
- Further reading: *Living Stones Pilgrimage with the Christians of the Holy Land*, Alison Hilliard & Betty Jane Bailey (Cassell UK). This is the most up-to-date book for pilgrims and is endorsed both by the Church in Jerusalem and by the Middle East Council of Churches.

Do we really recognize the ecumenical movement as the work of the Spirit?

Study 2 *Sending us to each other*

Keynote readings

Acts 6.1–7

Acts 8.26–40

Acts 11.19–30

Acts 16.1–15

Acts 20.17–28

AIM

To explore the meaning of the word 'mission' and to see the Spirit at work in today's encounters.

Way in

In pairs, look at the definitions on page 63 and select the one that challenges you most. Then come together and discuss what each pair has selected. Together write your own definition of mission for your local church.

Biblical reflection

Divide into two groups:

Group 1 to read Acts 6.1–7; 8.26–40; 11.19–30.

Group 2 to read Acts 16.1–15; 20.17–28.

● What part does the Holy Spirit play in each of these incidents?

Come together and share your findings.

What is the Holy Spirit saying to your church today? To your group?

● What is the Holy Spirit saying to your church today? To your group?

Welcome

Together read again Acts 16.11–15.

Reflect on the significance of the welcome Paul was given. Then read Matthew 10.5–14 and 40–42, and count the number of times the word 'welcome' (or 'receive') is used.

● What can we learn from these sayings of Jesus to improve the quality of our mission in the place where we live?

Reflect on the significance of 'welcome': who has been sent to you (or your church) in recent years — ministers, lay people, strangers...? What gifts of the Spirit have they brought? How have these gifts been received and used?

PRAYER

Holy Spirit,

who gave birth to the Church,

transform us into a family

where all are accepted in your love.

The Church exists by mission as fire exists by burning.
Emil Brunner

In Brazil, every Christian is a missionary.
You can be a missionary in your own neighbourhood.
Magali do Nascimento Cunha

I was made wonderfully welcome, and that is what changed me.
Margaret Shepherd

When I see a missionary I see a person who is away from home because of Jesus Christ.
DT Niles, Sri Lanka

A vision for the church

A Christian community that offers the hope, healing and caring love of God, so that people of all ages will want to be part of it.

Nourished through worship, prayer and teaching, we will reach out to one another, to the community and the world, knowing that we need to receive as well as to give.

Redhill Methodist Church

The Mission of the church is
- *to proclaim the good news of the Kingdom*
- *to teach, baptise and nurture new believers*
- *to respond to human need by loving service*
- *to seek to transform the unjust structures of society*
- *to strive to safeguard the integrity of creation and sustain and renew the life of the earth.*

The Five Marks of Mission — Anglican Consultative Council

63

Open our minds to the truths of holy scripture:
that community is built when all are welcome —
not when the poor learn from the rich,
or the weak from the strong —
but when the strong learn from the weak,
the rich from the poor,
adults from the insights of children,
the able from the disabled,
the sighted from those with impaired vision...
In receiving one another, may we be transformed
into the community of your vision.

Keynote readings
Ezekiel 37.1–14
Mark 4.35–41
Romans 8.12–17
Galatians 5.16–26
Galatians 6.1–10
Ephesians 6.10–20
Revelation 3.14–22

Study 3 *Giving life*

AIM

To explore and be open to ways in which the Spirit gives life.

After the storm

Ask the group to imagine themselves as disciples of Jesus in the boat with him when the storm blew up on Lake Galilee. Encourage them to enter into the experience, as you read the story — Mark 4.35–41. The small fishing vessel is over-towered by waves six to eight feet high. You are drenched by the spray and powerless against the wind. And Jesus is asleep...

How do you feel? Think your way through the experience to the eventual calm. Discuss your feelings.

What has had to give way so that the breath of God may bring calm?

If some of the group are willing to share personal experiences, share with one another times of suffering and despair when peace has come after the storm. Peace rarely comes automatically. What has had to give way so that the breath of God may bring calm?

Think of areas of the world where there is now peace where once there was conflict and war. By what processes has the Spirit worked to restore the life of the people?

Reflect together on the work of the Spirit in the light of the following words:

'If I had not suffered
I would not have known the love of God.
If many people had not suffered
God's love would not have been passed on.
If Jesus had not suffered
God's love would not have been made visible.'

Mizuno Genzo, Japan

Life for dry bones

Again ask the group to put themselves in others' shoes: to think back to the 6th century BC and imagine that they are Jewish exiles in Babylon. Forty years have gone by. Many of those who experienced the terrible war which caused them to be deported have already died and the younger generation have no memories of life in Judah to inspire them. The people have lost hope, and many are indifferent. Life in Babylon isn't so bad after all. Some Jews have started businesses and done well for themselves. The dream of returning home has faded. The faith of their ancestors is no longer alive.

Read to them the words of the prophet in Ezekiel 37.1–14.

What feelings do they evoke? What are their initial responses? What changes will a return to Judah make to them?

Read the passage again, but this time think of your own situation — your life — your church — your neighbourhood.

● Where do you see the Spirit wanting to breathe new life?

Fruits of the Spirit

Read Galatians 5.16–26. Reflect on the fruits of the Spirit together with the words of Jesus, 'By their fruit you will recognize them' *(Matthew 7.20)*.

PRAYER

Holy Spirit,
cooling and refreshing breeze,
moving within us
as you first moved

Where do you see the Spirit wanting to breathe new life?

on the face of the waters,
fill us and refresh us
with your all-pervading presence.

Holy Spirit,
fire of God,
burning within the hearts of prophets
until they cry out against injustice,
cleanse us of insularity
and reluctance to protest when evil prospers.

Holy Spirit —
rushing wind, unconfined,
blowing where you will across the world,
sweeping us up with your power,
raging,
buffeting,
causing havoc,
uprooting what has stood for centuries,
pulling us on,
turning us inside out with new insights,
preventing us from standing still,
leading us into all truth,
impelling us to move with you
across all boundaries,
bringing peace, unity and reconciliation —
empower and renew us
and do not allow us
to resist your direction.

ACTION

Is there a new challenge from any of the studies in this book that the Holy Spirit is making to you as a group? Decide together what you can do to allow new life to grow.

Holy Spirit —
do not allow us
to resist your
direction

WORKING FOR A BETTER WORLD

Study 1 *Return and Renewal*

AIM

To calculate the cost of rebuilding a better world.

Preparation

1. *You will need a game of Snakes and Ladders, or — if you do not have one and are not able to borrow one — make an enlarged copy of the game on page 68.*

2. *Make photocopies of the questions on page 69, and of the affirmation below, for each member of the group.*

Keynote readings
Nehemiah 1.1–11
Nehemiah 4.1–9
Nehemiah 5.1–13

Going back

Set out and draw attention to the board game Snakes and Ladders. If time permits play the game for a while. Invite members to reflect on the progress of life so far, listing low points under a column headed 'Snakes' and high points under 'Ladders'. This should be done individually. Be aware that some of their 'snakes' may relate to experiences which are painful to recall. Without placing any pressure on anyone, offer the opportunity to share with the group the story behind a 'snake' or a 'ladder'. After a period of silence read aloud Psalm 139 verses 1–3, 7–12. Give each member a copy of the affirmation below and invite the group to say it together.

An act of affirmation

At the pinnacles of achievement and success,
In the depths of failure, grief or despair,
In all our hopes to rise,
And in our fears to fall,
God knows us and loves us;
God forgives and renews us;
God never leaves us nor forsakes us.
Thanks be to God for this unfailing care.

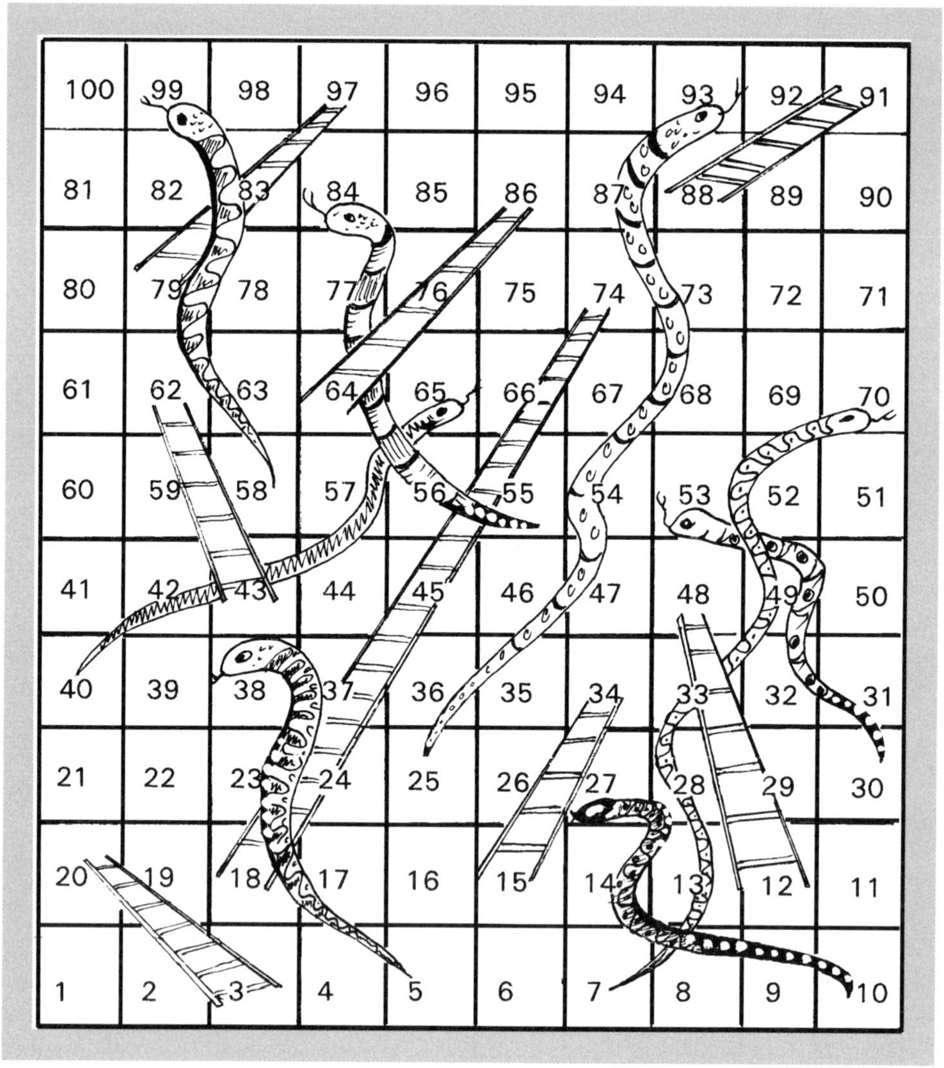
100 99 98 97 96 95 94 93 92 91
81 82 83 84 85 86 87 88 89 90
80 79 78 77 76 75 74 73 72 71
61 62 63 64 65 66 67 68 69 70
60 59 58 57 56 55 54 53 52 51
41 42 43 44 45 46 47 48 49 50
40 39 38 37 36 35 34 33 32 31
21 22 23 24 25 26 27 28 29 30
20 19 18 17 16 15 14 13 12 11
1 2 3 4 5 6 7 8 9 10

IF I WERE...

Imagine you are the person named and try to complete each sentence on his/her behalf. What feelings lie behind each statement? Mark each one with an 'S' for 'snake' or an 'L' for 'ladder', according to what it might represent to the person concerned — or 'SL' if you think it is potentially both a 'snake' and a 'ladder'.

1. A successful business person: 'I could not manage without...

2. A refugee seeking political asylum in another country: 'I cannot go back because...

3. A prisoner of conscience/political hostage: 'I felt encouraged when...

4. The Secretary of State for Northern Ireland: 'I stand firm in my commitment to the Peace Process in spite of... because...

5. A homeless, unemployed young person: 'I don't think it is fair that...

6. A peasant farmer: 'My life would be easier if...

7. The King of Jordan: 'I feel challenged by...

8. A low-paid immigrant worker in the UK: 'I feel angry when....

9. A 10 year old child watching the television news. 'I don't understand why...

10. Yourself: 'The world would be a better place if...

Moving on

Give everyone a photocopy of the exercise on the previous page. Stress that first thoughts are preferable; the exercise need not be completed in full (allow 5–8 minutes).

Then, as a group, invite members to share their feelings about attempting this exercise. Read some of the keynote readings together and note some of the ups and downs associated with Nehemiah's return to rebuild Jerusalem. What can we learn from this about rebuilding the world today?

Encourage members to be realistic in calculating the cost of such actions in terms of their use of time, money, resources, personal commitment/ sacrifice, a change of heart, coping with what others might say or think...

Snakes into ladders

In the light of this discussion and the group's earlier feelings about their own 'snakes' and 'ladders', invite members to suggest one action they would be prepared to take —

— alone;

— with others in their local church;

— in support of political/economic measures initiated by their government —

to change a 'snake' into a 'ladder' in one of the situations described. Encourage members to be realistic in calculating the cost of such actions in terms of their use of time, money, resources, personal commitment/sacrifice, a change of heart, coping with what others might say or think...

PRAYER

Most high and holy God,

help us to aspire to be the best that we can be,

to want the best for all your people,

whatever the cost.

Down-to-earth God,

dwelling among us in Jesus Christ,

do not let us forget all that you have done for us. Amen

For next week

Try to list five positive qualities/attitudes which can build up good human relationships and five negative attitudes which can break them down. Bring your list to the meeting.

Study 2 *Back to basics*

AIM

To identify the tools needed for the task of building community.

Preparation

● Prepare a large chart with the outline of a brick wall drawn on it, and small cards representing bricks corresponding in scale to those drawn on your chart. You will also need some blu-tak or double-sided sticky tape.

● Make photocopies of the poem 'Deconstructing disability' on page 73, to enable some preparation for the next study.

Firm foundations

Nehemiah was challenged, not only to rebuild a city but to restore the faith of his people and renew a real sense of community. We will now explore the positive attitudes/qualities that we need today to respond to that same challenge.

Give each member pieces of card cut into brick shapes and small pieces of blu-tak or double-sided sticky tape. Ask them in turn to name a positive attitude from the list they were invited to bring to the meeting and to say why they consider this to be helpful in building up good relationships in the family, at work, at church or in the wider community. Encourage the group to think of one word to describe each quality listed. For each positive quality named and agreed by the group, write a word on one of the bricks and place it on the wall. Ask one member to read out the list of positive qualities from Galatians 5.22–25. Compare these with the word bricks already on the wall. Allow time for discussion and addition/deletion of bricks in the light of the discussion.

● How can we help one another to cultivate and display these qualities?

● What help do we need to teach our children to value them?

● Does the church have a role in this?

Keynote readings
Nehemiah 6.1–16
Nehemiah 8.1–3; 9–18
Nehemiah 13.23–31
Galatians 5.13–25

How can we help one another to cultivate and display these qualities?

71

Attitudes that undermine

Repeat the listing and brick-labelling exercise in relation to the negative attitudes identified by each member. Ask another group member to read aloud the negative attitudes listed in Galatians 5.19–21. Repeat the comparison exercise allowing time for addition/deletion of bricks. Ask members to share experiences of the ways in which their efforts to build up community have been undermined by some of the negative attitudes identified and displayed on the wall.

● How can we help one another to replace negative with positive bricks? Remove from the wall all the negative bricks.

Spend some time in silence looking at the wall and considering whether or not it is capable of standing. Ask each member to write on the reverse side of one negative brick, an action s/he would be prepared to take to reverse its undermining effect and then replace it in the wall.

Christ, the Master Builder, Cornerstone of our faith, take the raw materials of our lives and fashion them anew for your service

PRAYER

God our Creator,
you have made us and all your people
in your own image.
You have shown us the qualities you want us to display
to build up our life together in your world.
Forgive us when we undermine your good foundations
or allow other people or unexpected problems
to shake our certainties and cause our courage to crumble.
Christ, the Master Builder,
Cornerstone of our faith,
take the raw materials of our lives
and fashion them anew for your service.
Spirit, the leveller, rest upon us
to keep us upright and straight. Amen

For next week

Give each member a copy of the poem 'Deconstructing Disability'. Ask them to read it and try to identify 'snakes' and

Study 3 *People with disabilities*

AIM

To understand our own and other people's limitations.

Keynote reading
Luke 13.10–17

Deconstructing disability

Because they could not see
the scars on my spine
my 'orange badge' became
something to explain,
no passport to freedom
but a source of pain.
Because they could not see
the scars on my spine
their disability
complicated mine.

Because they could not feel
my back-grinding pain,
I used to feign a limp
in the disabled bays
which spoiled my shopping trips,
even on good days.
Because they could not feel
my back-grinding pain,
my disability
was a hidden bane.

Because they cannot know
unless I explain,
how pain can disable
the body and the soul,
my silence still colludes
in paying the toll.
Because they cannot know
unless I explain,
OUR DISABILITIES
will always remain.

Hidden disabilities

1. What is the hidden physical disability of the author?

Because they
could not see
the scars on
my spine
their disability
complicated
mine

73

Is there a 'hidden' element in all disabilities — physical, emotional and mental?

2. How would you characterize the nature of 'their disability' in verse 1?

3. Why do you think that the author felt the need to 'feign a limp'?

4. List ways in which you think the author experienced both physical and mental pain.

5. How could some of the author's mental pain have been avoided?

6. How do you think that the author could have explained the physical and mental pain to someone with no experience of such things?

7. How appropriate is it to attempt such explanations?

8. To what extent are all disabilities 'OURS' — i.e. shared?

9. Is there a 'hidden' element in all disabilities — physical, emotional and mental?

10. Imagine that you have one of the following disabilities and suggest ways in which you might try to communicate your special needs to someone who knows nothing about it:

DEAFNESS; TINNITUS; CHRONIC DEPRESSION; DYSLEXIA; EPILEPSY; ANGINA; CHRONIC BACK PAIN.

Together, in plenary discussion, encourage members to say which questions they found most difficult to answer and why. If there is a lack of knowledge about any of the disabilities listed, suggest that members make contact with local support or advocacy groups to find out more.

'Bent by unbending ways'

Read aloud Luke 13.10–17.

● Why did Jesus draw attention to the woman by calling to her?

● How do you think she felt when he did this?

● Why did the president of the synagogue feel threatened by what Jesus did? Were his expressed reasons the real ones?

● What other feelings might he have been experiencing?

● What can we learn from this story about openness and

flexibility in our attitude to our own and other people's apparent or hidden disabilities?

● Can you see any parallels between the human interactions in this story and those of the poem?

PRAYER

Enabling God,

Help all your people

to bear the wounds

of being exposed to your liberating love.

Do not let us be disabled by real or imagined burdens,

disempowered by real or imagined threats to our status or security,

disturbed by real or imagined fears.

Untie all our bonds, save those that bind us to one another

and to you. Amen

For further reflection

In the life and worship of your local church, what are the 'snakes' that could put disabled people down? Where are the 'ladders' that might lift them up?

For next week

Try to imagine how you would feel if your own health, or that of someone close to you, was threatened by any of the following: HIV/AIDS; Multiple Sclerosis; Crohn's Disease/Colitis; Eczema/Psoriasis; Schizophrenia.

STUDY 4 *Health for all*

AIM

To explore ways of keeping spiritually fit.

Keynote readings
Mark 1.40–45
Mark 5.1–20

Touching the untouchable

Display the list of illnesses from last week.

● Does anyone want to add to it?

● How far do these illnesses represent modern equivalents of those that were shunned or feared at the time of Christ?

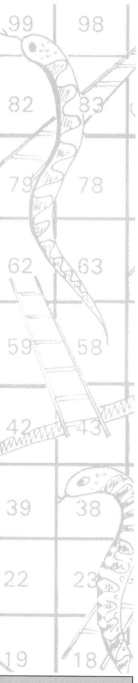

● What do members know about each illness listed? Make a note of any that are unfamiliar.

Naming fears

● Why do people fear these illnesses?
● What problems do they present to:
   1. those who are ill?
   2. people who care for them?
   3. family and friends?
   4. the community?

We shall overcome

● What changes of attitude, thought, and behaviour are needed if these fears are to be overcome by the four categories of people named above?

A spiritual keep-fit exercise

Compose a *'Snakes and Ladders'* prayer based on the discussion. For each illness on the agreed list, cut out a card or paper snake. Write the name of the illness on one side and the associated fears and problems on the reverse. Cut out rectangles to represent the rungs of a ladder — one for each agreed change. Write one change on each rung. Ensure that everyone can see the display area/table. Distribute the cards randomly. Invite members to participate by placing the cards in the display area and joining in the reading and responses, as follows:

SNAKES

Leader   Our fears are like 'snakes lurking in the grass'.

All   *Help us to look at them and name them'.*

Leader   Loving God, we pray for those who feel or are made to feel unlovely, unclean, untouchable.

           For people with... *(Each person who lays down a snake card should now read out the illness named on it.)*

Leader   Caring God, teach us that love casts out fear; show us how to see people not problems.
           (Each snake card should be turned over in silence.)

LADDERS

Leader   Our longings and good intentions
          are like ladders of opportunity
          and growth.

All   **Help us to hold on to them and use them.**

          *In silence, each rung of the ladder is put in place
          as the cards are displayed. Follow with a period of
          silence or shared intercession according to the
          group response.*

Leader   Healing God, you alone can make us whole.
              Change our hearts;
              change our minds;
              change our ways.

All   **As we renew our commitment to one another
          and to you.** *Amen*

For further action

Collect information about local and national support or
advocacy groups related to any of the illnesses with which
you felt unfamiliar.

For next week

*Bring to the meeting a press cutting/magazine picture which for
you symbolizes emptiness or fullness.*

Study 5 *Bread is for sharing*

AIM

To investigate strategies for sharing.

Food for thought

Place a partially filled glass of water in the centre of the
group.

● Is it half empty or half full?

It depends on how we see it. Ask members to indicate
which answer they would have given.

Invite members in turn to display and comment briefly on
the images of 'emptiness' and 'fullness' that they have
brought.

Have a few of your own available in case anyone has

Keynote readings
Genesis 18.1–15
I Kings 17.8–24
Philippians 2.1–9

forgotten, e.g. a starving child, a very slim fashion model, a grief-stricken parent, devastated crops, a colourful food picture, a pregnant woman, a happy party scene...

Explore reactions to the images
● Who might feel guilty, angry, envious, marginalized, upset, happy, defensive, encouraged, hopeful, in response to any of them?
● What other feelings/responses might they provoke?
● How far are any of these reactions conditioned by circumstances beyond our or other people's control?

Emptiness into fullness
Choose an emptiness picture. To CHANGE THIS, consider:
● What could I give or give up?
● What can my church do or say?
● What other actions or responses are needed?

Who are the 'strangers' who might change us if we let them into our homes, our hearts, our lives?

Loaves and wishes
Look at the keynote readings.
● What can we learn from them about the hospitality and hope that can change emptiness into fullness? And the laughter of cynicism into the delight of shared hope?
● Who are the 'strangers' who might change us if we let them into our homes, our hearts, our lives?
● Who are the 'widows' whose generosity shames us?
● Who are the 'prophets' who challenge us?

Further food for thought
Think about ways in which food imagery is used in talk about money, ambitions etc. 'Bread', 'Dough', 'Lolly', 'Gravy', 'having our cake and eating it', 'wanting our bread buttered on both sides'...
● What does this reveal about attitudes and expectations?

ACTION
● Find out about alternative barter/exchange schemes where skills and time are shared and no payment made.
● Is there a scheme like this in your area?

● How would you persuade people to set one up?
● What makes such schemes work?

PRAYER

In silence, reflect on Philippians 2.1–9.

Self-emptying God,
fill us with your generosity of spirit,
that we may find satisfaction and give satisfaction
in sharing according to need. Amen

For next week
Ask each member to bring some food or drink for a shared meal.

Further reading
Loaves and Wishes, ed. Antonia Till (Virago, London, 1992). Published to celebrate Oxfam's fiftieth anniversary. Full of witty, challenging and moving writing on food and food-related issues. Recipes for meals; recipes for change; much food for thought.

Self-emptying God, fill us with your generosity of spirit

Study 6 *Bread and circuses*

Note: *This week is different. There is a choice of aims and activities. Over a simple shared meal allow members to explore their options and come to a decision. Groups that have reacted cautiously to any of the exercises in previous weeks will probably choose Aim 1. Risk-takers may be prepared to go for Aim 2. Do not pressurize people. Allow enough time to explore what people think and feel.*

AIM 1
To work out how dreams can become realities.

AIM 2
To devise a board game based on 'One World' issues.

Stress that Aim 1 involves Bible study and discussion. Aim 2 requires creativity, imagination and action.

If Aim 1 is selected proceed as follows
The Roman Satirist, Juvenal (c. AD 60–130) said of the citizen of those days that 'there were only two things that he worried about or longed for — bread and circuses' (i.e.

Keynote readings
(for both aims)
Acts 2.42–47
Romans 12.9–13

Why did the early Church's experiment in communal living fail?

the 'big match' — the games in the arena).

1. Is this still true of the average citizen today?
2. What are the things s/he worries about?
3. What does s/he long for? Compile a list.
4. Look at the ideals and ethics described in the readings.
5. Are they impossible dreams or realistic goals?
6. How do they compare with the 'worries' and 'longings' lists?
7. Why did the early Church's experiment in communal living fail?
8. What can we learn from this and any other attempts at 'having all things in common' of which members may have experience/information?

For Aim 2 proceed thus

Drawing on material from Studies 1–5 devise a 'Snakes and Ladders' type board game that could be used in your neighbourhood to raise funds for a project in your community or in another part of the world.

1. Establish the rules of the game.
2. Prepare 6 identity cards for the players and a selection of 'snake' and 'ladder' cards relating to ups or downs that each player might encounter when landing on a corresponding square in the game.
3. Decide how and where such a game might be used: how you would publicize the event, who would compère it, and what extra help you might need.

Encourage members to stretch their imaginations and have FUN!

PRAYER and ACTION (for both aims)

Enabling God — nothing is impossible with you.

Support us when we take risks or dare to dream.

Stand by us when we try something new.

Give us the courage to turn good ideas into good practice. Amen

Sample cards to stimulate ideas:

You are an illegal immigrant called Rosa aged 30.
Your family live in the Philippines.
You work as a chambermaid in a North Wales hotel.
You try to send money back home regularly.

IDENTITY CARD

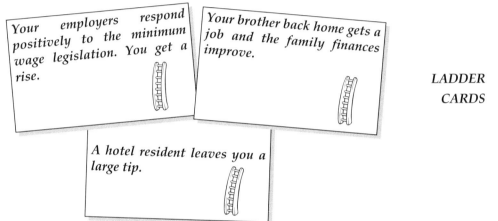

Your employers respond positively to the minimum wage legislation. You get a rise.

Your brother back home gets a job and the family finances improve.

LADDER CARDS

A hotel resident leaves you a large tip.

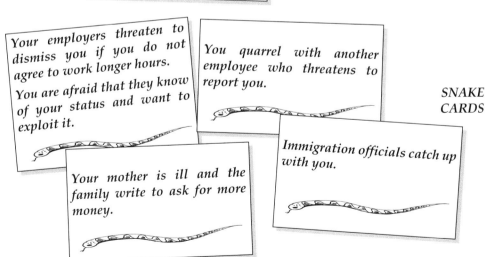

Your employers threaten to dismiss you if you do not agree to work longer hours. You are afraid that they know of your status and want to exploit it.

You quarrel with another employee who threatens to report you.

SNAKE CARDS

Immigration officials catch up with you.

Your mother is ill and the family write to ask for more money.

Try to ensure that the identity cards cover a wide range of age, ethnicity and personal circumstances with snake and ladder cards appropriate to each.

BUILDING COMMUNITY

Notes for the leader

This series of studies concentrates on building relationships within the church community, and we will symbolize this by building a model of a church. Select a sturdy foundation box and on it print the theme 'Building community'. Each week a smaller box, labelled with the week's thought, can be added. The boxes will emphasize the idea of building and be a reminder each week of previous studies.

Look ahead and make sure you have ten smaller boxes, one for each study. If you really want to make a construction that looks like a church, you will of course need more! Or you could do this on a smaller scale with Lego/Duplo bricks (borrowed from children you know) and self-adhesive labels.

In addition you will need:

● for **Study 2** — one central candle, a smaller candle for each group member and a safe receptacle in which to place lighted candles; some quiet music; some slips of paper.

● for **Study 3** — a large sheet of paper, a fibre tip pen and small slips of paper.

● for **Study 4** — ask members to bring a reminder of the past – a theatre ticket, a photograph, a piece of domestic equipment, an old newspaper...

● for **Study 5** — invite someone to talk about people who are often excluded by communities (e.g. the housebound elderly, drug addicts, battered women, a refugee...)

● for **Study 6** — greetings cards for members to sign.

● for **Study 7** — make arrangements to see a video about marriage — maybe a short sequence from a film where the meaning of marriage is questioned or highlighted — or invite someone to speak to your group.

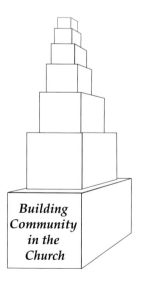

*Building
Community
in the
Church*

Study 1 *Building community in church*

AIM
To take time to appreciate the gathered community in church.

Keynote readings
1 Corinthians 1.10–17
1 Corinthians 3.1–23

Introducing the theme
Introduce the base or foundation box for the theme labelled, 'Building community in church'.

Discuss: On Sunday we gather together for worship — but how well do we know each other?

Take time for members of the group to chat informally. Where do they usually sit in church and what do they see as their special contribution in worship? Do not allow anyone to be 'just' something. All are equally important (intercessor, singer, steward, reader, preacher, notices secretary, junior church leader...).

Worship brings us all together — but is there one facet of church life to which individuals feel especially committed? *(Allow ONE per person.)* Again, invite informal conversations and then a full group sharing.

Do we respect and affirm one another in our 'calling'? How important is this in building community?

A sense of belonging?
Read together 1 Corinthians 3.10–23.

Make a list of the ways in which members of the group see themselves contributing to their church community. Together these activities/responsibilities help to create a sense of belonging.

● How can we ensure that Christ is central in our commitment? When might we be tempted to build on other foundations?

Read 1 Corinthians 1.10–17 and 3.1–9 where Paul is talking about the importance we tend to give to personalities in the church.

● Are there tensions which arise between different facets of church life? You could use the list you made for reference!

● Do we respect and affirm one another in our 'calling'? How important is this in building community?

To Paul the Apostle from ......, a servant in the church of...

From Paul the Apostle to the church at... Greetings, grace and peace...

Adding to the model

Decide together what you will write on your first box/brick and place it on your foundation base of your model church.

Correspondence with a contemporary Paul!

Divide into two groups. With the help of 1 Corinthians, invite:

Group A to write a letter to a '21st Century Paul', about the challenges and problems of your church;

Group B to write a letter from Paul to your church community about some of the problems that trouble you.

If time does not allow for this, the exercise can be continued at the start of the next session. The leader may choose to provide light refreshments to mark the end of the group work, and then ask for the letters to be read later on. Or they can be read at the beginning of the next session. Receive both with thanks.

PRAYER

We thank you for this time together;

for the reminder that we are all valued members of your church community.

We thank you for the skills and energies that are given in your service.

We think of other members of our church communities, not represented here, but on whom we rely in order that your community is whole.

We pray for ourselves, that we may play our part well and that all that we do may be to your honour and glory.

Bless us in the coming week and may our lives prove to be a blessing to others. In your name we offer ourselves to you. Amen

Keynote readings
1 Corinthians 10.14–11.1
1 Corinthians 1.17–29
1 Corinthians 12.1–31
1 Corinthians 13.1–13

Study 2 *Living as a scattered community*

AIM

To recognize the everyday challenges that Christian commitment brings, and a variety of solutions which may prove useful.

From the last study
If you didn't have time to do this last week, read your letters to or from a contemporary Paul to one another.

Reflection
Last week you looked at your own role in the local church and how this linked with other members. As a reminder, lay the first 'building block' on the foundation box of your model church.

Next, invite a period of silent reflection (perhaps with some quiet background music), to reflect on each day since your last meeting. Give each person a strip of paper and ask them to write one word to describe a significant part/activity of each of the last seven days, e.g. work, holiday, letter, news, forgiveness, conversation...

After this, and continuing at a personal level, guide the group to think of how belonging to a Christian community influenced any of the situations they recalled. Allow time for quiet reflection.

Relevance
Ask each person to select one incident from their list that they would be willing to share with the group.

After the sharing, ask: How does the community of the Church help us in our lives every day?

Read together and reflect on 1 Corinthians 13.1–13.

Look together at the challenge in 1 Corinthians 11.1 'Be imitators of me — as I am of Christ.' What does this mean for us?

Adding to the model
Think of a word to write on your second block and add this to your model church.

Draw the meeting to a close in subdued lighting or candlelight if practical. Arrange and light a central candle and give each individual an unlighted candle (or night-light).

PRAYER
'Do everything to the glory of God' —
Loving God, we come before you,

How does the community of the Church help us in our lives every day?

grateful for this time together,
glad to be able to reflect on a week gone by,
humbled to think that you have been with us
every step of the way.
We thank you for the wise words
and thoughtful actions of other people toward us,
for the ways they have reflected to us your love and care.
Forgive our blindness and lack of trust,
our negative thoughts and minimum effort.
Forgive us when we let you down,
and blur your image in other people's eyes and hearts.

Help us to love you more dearly, and follow you more nearly,
reflecting your image wherever we go and whatever we do.

Invite members to light their candles from the central candle and to hold their thoughts in silence.

When this is completed, keep silence for a few moments.

Read 1 Corinthians 10.14 to 11.1.

Pause

End by sharing the Grace together.

Study 3 *What are the challenges?*

Keynote readings
1 Corinthians
14.13–33
1 Corinthians 15.1–19,
35–44

AIM

To draw out of 1 Corinthians qualities for building today's church community.

Reflection
Reflect on the beginnings of your model church and the words you have written on each piece.

Today's study is about identifying challenges, problems and joys included in that letter from Paul to a young Church.

Challenges and joys
Divide into pairs, and share among them the following readings from 1 Corinthians:

1.10–31	3.10–17
4.9–13	10.14–33
11.1–34	14.13–33
15.1–19, 35–44	

Give each pair a piece of paper. Ask them to divide the paper into two columns under the headings CHALLENGES and JOYS. Ask them to work through the readings and note down the challenges and joys Paul describes. *Allow plenty of time.*

Together as a group make a 'common' list. Discuss:

● What does this say about problems and joys in the church today?

● What causes the greatest divisions?

● What doubts are prevalent, and how can we address them?

● Was it helpful for the Corinthians to have Paul's counsel?

● Did Paul help to build community?

● Do we have an equivalent today?

Adding to the model
What word will you write on today's building block, and how will you symbolize today's sharing together?

Building Community in the Church

PRAYER

As a closing prayer for today, use the hymn, 'Jesus calls us o'er the tumult'. End by saying the Lord's Prayer and sharing the Grace.

Study 4 *No generation gap*

AIM

To recognize that not all divisions in the Church are across generations.

Keynote readings
Deuteronomy 4.1–2, 6–10
Mark 3.31–35
Mark 9.33–37
Luke 2.41–52
1 Timothy 4.6 to 5.2

Preparation
Place your model building, as it is so far, in a place that is easily visible, and prepare a similar place for members to put their contributions together to build up a historical picture.

Discourage them from talking about their items before the meeting.

Relics that tell a story
On my hearth at home, there sits a 'flat iron'. I have never used it for the job for which it was created. It was an indispensable part of the household for my mother-in-law

What would you put in a time capsule to tell the story of your belief and involvement as members of the Church?

before electricity was installed in her home. An electric iron then made it redundant. The flat iron is a reminder of a past era. If it could speak, it would tell of its work and worth to the family as it was heated on the embers of the fire in order to iron out the creases of bed linen and clothes.

This iron symbolizes the changes within the home and work-place in the last century. They are almost beyond comprehension! Pause for people to add their own reminiscences, and to place their contributions together. Allow time to appreciate their significance, and encourage individuals to talk about them.

In the same way, from oral descriptions to carefully kept diaries, the Gospels are invaluable to us as Christians, reminding us of our reason for being a church.

In Britain today, fewer people value their family roots. The last century has brought greater mobility than ever before. It has also brought a different understanding of family values and a different set of values by which to measure 'success'. To a button-pressing, computer-literate, technology-minded generation, the telephone and handwriting seem to be becoming irrelevant. Yet both are capable of good communication.

● It is often said that the Church does not change. Do you think that this is true? Think of examples — new versions of the Bible, new ways of worship, liturgies, new styles of leadership, music, songs, instruments, language... Do these enhance or threaten? Why? Who prefers which?

● Can you put an age (generation) on them?

● What does this say about this week's theme?

Read Deuteronomy 4.1–2, 6–10.

● What are the important things that you would want to pass on to the next generation?

● What would you put in a time capsule to tell the story of your belief and involvement as members of the Church?

Read Mark 3.31–35 and Mark 9.33–37.

● What pointers does Jesus give to overcoming the generation gap?

Adding to the model

Add the next block to your model church and write on it a phrase which sums up today's discussion.

PRAYER

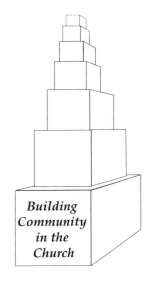

Building Community in the Church

Lord God, by whom all change is wrought,
By whom new things to birth are brought,
In whom no change is known;
Whate'er thou dost, whate'er thou art,
Thy people still in thee have part;
Still, still thou art our own.

Spirit, who makest all things new,
Thou leadest onward; we pursue
The heavenly march sublime.
'Neath thy renewing fire we glow,
And still from strength to strength we go,
From height to height we climb.

Thomas Hornblower Gill (1819–1906)

Go in peace, strong in the knowledge that God loves us and goes with us. Amen

Study 5 *No one excluded*

AIM

To be honest about our exclusivity.

Setting the scene

Look at your building model so far and add perhaps one historical object that has some relevance.

One of the difficulties of using a building as a model of the church is that it has walls and therefore a limited capacity.

In what ways are we 'exclusive' in the Church? Language, jargon, groups, patterns of worship, decision-making, times of meeting, places of meeting. Feel free to add or delete from the list.

Think of examples:

— homeless people may be asleep on church steps;

— unemployed and redundant people can be seen playing cards on the church steps;

— the church doors are locked...

Keynote readings
Mark 10.13–16
Luke 14.15–24
John 4.5–24
Galatians 3.28
James 2.1–10, 14–17

89

A ministry of welcome

Expecting commitment from church members is often seen as old-fashioned. It is demanded at work; that is enough. People are less willing to commit themselves to groups than they once were. Why is this?

Statistically, socially, most people's community is centred around work rather than where they live. The community base is on the move, having implications for family, spouses and leisure-time. We are thrown on the defensive. We talk of hazards and risks and yet no one is excluded by Jesus. Where is the good news — declared by Jesus — for all?

Are we surprised when people step across the threshold of the Church? How do we welcome them?

● Are we surprised when people step across the threshold of the Church? How do we welcome them?

This is a very sensitive and skilled task. We must be careful to be warm in our welcome, but not patronizing; open and inclusive but not so enthusiastic as to be assuming or suffocating!

In pairs look at the following verses:

John 4.5–24

Luke 24.13–52

Matthew 14.14–21

Mark 10.13–16

Are there examples we can follow from Jesus' methods? Think of other examples.

Difficult questions

Think of groupings from which

a) you feel excluded

b) you prefer to be excluded.

Take time to think properly about these categories.

● What opportunities are there to learn and share with exclusive communities? E.g. prison, residential homes, hospitals, hospices, differently-abled people?

● How many things do we exclude ourselves from in order to be voluntarily employed within the church community?

● Should the church community be outgoing in order to assist and learn from those who feel marginalized and excluded by others' actions?

- Should the church go to them and meet them on their own terms?
- Is it possible now to hear from someone working with an 'excluded' group of people?

Give plenty of time for these questions and receive any suggestions for possible follow-up: e.g. a visit or raising an appropriate suggestion on a church council agenda or whatever.

Adding to the model
Before you add the next building block to your model church think carefully what slogan you will write on it — e.g. ALL WELCOME 0–100 YEARS...

PRAYER

We thank you, Lord,

for helping us to look at uncomfortable questions.

We know very well what you would do,

but then you didn't have church structure and fabric to maintain.

You concentrated on your Father's will

and improved the fabric of people's everyday life.

Forgive us if we hide away in the church

when we should be out breaking taboos

and cutting red tape to enlarge our vision

and show your love in action

to people long-denied that quality of life.

Help us not to make excuses

or to compartmentalize people in our minds.

Keep making us feel uncomfortable if we stereotype

and make decisions for people who could be helped to make their own.

So use this session to prod us into wider action with the support of our church community.

We offer ourselves again to you. Amen

How many things do we exclude ourselves from in order to be voluntarily employed within the church community?

91

Study 6 *Forgetting self*

AIM

To look at ways of losing one's hold on oneself, and so focusing on others through the example of Jesus.

Focusing our minds

We begin this session by spending time recognizing what we have been doing today in order, then, to forget and focus on our subject.

Give everyone a slip of paper to list what they have been doing earlier in the day... preparing food, shopping, cleaning, visiting, computing, walking, searching for something, work...

After a time of quiet, pray:

O God, we stop our busyness to come into this group.

Thank you for today, for all the things we've been able to do...

(Invite the group to offer, from their lists, one activity in turn until all the items they have written down have been mentioned.)

We thank you for the work that has been done;

for all the encounters that have taken place,

and experiences that have lifted us out of our own set pattern

and drawn our attention to someone else's needs and cares.

We pause to think again of all the activities we have named.

Forgive us if what we have done has not been worthy of our calling.

We stop and think of one conversation we have shared today,

or some time in the last week,

and offer a silent prayer for that person.

Now, loving Lord, we pray for your continuing presence in this time together.

Continue to knit us together in community. Amen

Setting our own trends

Where do we take a measure for our lives? 'Keeping up with the Joneses' is tempting. Media advertising and telephone selling obviously pay or people would not be employed to do them. Advertising is carefully targeted to convince. Can we honestly say that we are exempt from this?

- Are there 'codes' which could help others to get through the expectation levels? E.g.
  —Fair Trade shopping and the attitude of always asking: Do I really need this?
  —refusing to use a credit card;
  —asking at whose expense is this cheap to me?
- Do these and similar methods help us in other aspects of our lives?
- Think of people in public life who have 'bucked the trend', who seem to have forgotten self-interest in order to improve and encourage a better way of life for someone else.
  E.g. David Blunkett, a blind Member of Parliament in Britain, has campaigned for the rights of children and education. He has proved that he can do a tough job despite not being able to see.
  Mo Mowlam, Secretary for Northern Ireland and British Member of Parliament, has championed the cause of Peace in that troubled country even though she has personally been undergoing treatment for a life -threatening disease.
  David Bellamy is an environmentalist whose name is 'household' in Britain but whose warning words in relation to the world's resources are proving to be timely and wise.
- Think of people in the life of the Church whose commitment have caused them to 'lose their hold on their own life', but help someone else's.
  E.g. Martin Luther King, Nelson Mandela, Rigoberta Menchu, Archbishop Oscar Romero...
- To whom would you award that accolade in your own church and community?

Biblical reflection
In pairs, look at the Bible readings listed in the margin. What further challenges do they make to us?

Bring this time of discussion to a close with the suggestion of finding a way of affirming/encouraging those you have thought of — perhaps by all signing greetings cards.

Think of people in public life who have forgotten self-interest in order to improve and encourage a better way of life for someone else. To whom would you award that accolade in your own church and community?

Adding to the model

Are there issues which have challenged you today? Identify one word to write on today's brick and add it to your model.

PRAYER

Close with a time of silent prayer and then the sharing of the Grace.

Study 7 *Honouring Marriage*

Keynote readings

Proverbs 31.10–31
Song of Solomon
2.8–13
1 Corinthians 5.1–14
1 Corinthians 6.12–20
1 Corinthians 7.1–40
1 Corinthians 13

AIM

To form a realistic definition of marriage.

Preparation

It would be interesting to invite an older couple and a comparatively newly married couple to reflect on the changing perceptions of marriage.

Another possibility may be to arrange to show a video on marriages within other faiths, or the conduct of marriage in other parts of the world.

Prayers could centre round The Marriage Service and the response made by the congregation in affirming the couple.

Visual aids might be a wedding ring, flowers, wine, and a prayer book.

The marriage at Cana

Read John 2.1–11. The marriage at Cana suggests a time of family celebration and imminent catastrophe that was avoided thanks to Mary's Son, Jesus, being present. The story is vividly recounted without any mention of the couple at the centre – the bride and groom.

● What is marriage? Take time to talk about marriage and agree a definition.

The way of excellence

Marriage is still assumed to be one of the practices that undergird community and family life. The most familiar passage associated with the Marriage Service is 1 Corinthians 13. Take time to read the passage and then discuss it verse by verse as a group.

- Which verse impresses you most?
- Which is the most difficult verse to live with in the twenty-first century?

Space in togetherness

In *The Prophet*, Kahlil Gibran speaks of marriage, and reflects poetically on 'space'. How important is space for a couple within marriage?

'Let there be spaces in your togetherness.

And let the winds of the heavens dance between you...

Give your hearts, but not into each other's keeping.

For only the hand of Life can contain your hearts.

And stand together yet not too near together:

For the pillars of the temples stand apart,

And the oak tree and the cypress grow not in each other's shadow.'

- Does this fit in with the definition you have agreed? How right is *The Prophet*?

Marriage in a changing society

Earlier in this series, attention was drawn to the change in social patterns *(Study 4)*.

- What pressures do these changes place within marriage?
- What additional threats are there to marriage?
  —Both couples working — probably spending more time with colleagues than each other — too much space?
  —Mortgage and other responsibilities.
  —Division of labour in the home.
  —Time for each other competes with social work/building community in work and possibly church activities too.
  —Children.
  —Ageing parents.
  —Expectations...

Make sure that singles, as well as couples, share their perspectives on these questions.

How important is space for a couple within marriage?

Adding to your model

What word or phrase will you add to your model? It might be covered in paper used for wrapping a wedding gift, or have a rose or ribbon on it to reflect the theme of marriage.

PRAYER

Give thanks for God's gifts of marriage and family life.
Pray for families where relationships are stressful;
for children who have particular problems within the family;
for older people, especially those who live alone;
that we may all find time to build upon our relationships with one another both in the family and the community.

Study 8 *Sharing suffering*

Keynote readings
Job 1.1–22
Job 2.1 to 3.26
Job 4.1–17
Job 5.5–27
Job 6.14–30
Job 7.7–21

AIM

To think of Job and put ourselves into his shoes.

Way in

Begin by singing or saying the hymn, 'Through all the changing scenes of life...'

The story of Job

Describe Job: an Arab — married — father — large family — farmer with plenty of livestock — owner — prosperous with servants — upright character — generous and caring — a man of faith, patience and endurance...

● What message did this image convey to people with regard to his belief in God? If God looks after his followers like this ... perhaps he's worth believing in?

Ask someone to read Job 1.6–22. Invite another member to list the contents of those verses as they are read. Then ask:

Who had the hardest task? The writer! Why? Because everything came thick and fast. Tragedy strikes Job in terms of his material life. Invite comments.

● How does Job cope?

● Does the story so far remind us of any experiences or

people we have known?

● What does this tell us of Job?

As if this is not enough... Read Job 2.1–10.

● Bad news travels fast and Job's friends come to see him. What would we say to Job, if we were in their place? Discuss.

What kind of God?

Read chapter 2 v.11–13 and reflect:

'If God's aim is to bring out the qualities of Job, this ploy too succeeds. Job's wife on earth plays the role of the 'adversary' in the heavenly assembly, but not even her words can touch his faith: 'Shall we accept good from God and not evil?' Despite this fervour, something within Job may have moved: he no longer speaks of 'the Eternal' but of 'the God', or simply 'God'. Rabbinic tradition distinguishes the names — the former represents God's compassion and love, the latter God's strict justice. Whatever the change may mean, Job's words hint at the bitter anger that will now spill out in the presence of his visitors.

Jonathan Magonet, Words for Today 2000 *(IBRA)*

Bad news travels fast and Job's friends come to see him. What would we say to Job, if we were in their place?

Testing our theories

Now have a time of personal reading to cover the other chapters listed in the margin.

● How do Job's friends react, and he to them? Theory and reality are not the same thing. What bearing does this have on Job and his friends?

'The global theory must inevitably ignore the individual circumstances. But it is not advisable to assert at the bedside the truths one thunders from the pulpit.' *(Jonathan Magonet*, Words for Today 2000)

● Can you think of examples where this has to be recognized today? E.g. when a generalization or theoretical stance has to be tempered in the hard reality of an individual dilemma — pregnancy, drugs, AIDS, divorce...

● Were there times when Jesus found himself doing the same? E.g. a Jew and a Samaritan woman, or the woman taken in adultery?

Adding to the model
Discuss what will symbolize today's session and prepare the block for your model. Should the paper be neat and tidy, or would something else be appropriate?

PRAYER

Living God, we thank you for your presence with us.

You know our thoughts before we think them,

You hear our words before we say them,

You read our minds before us.

Help us to pause in our busyness,

To meet people where they are,

To feel their need before they need to tell,

To be your Presence in person

As we go about our lives this week.

Say together the Blessing.

Study 9 *What is solidarity in suffering?*

AIM

Keynote readings
Job 8.1–22
Job 9.1–4
Job 10.1–15
Job 11.1–16
Job 13.6–23
Job 14.7–22
Job 19.13–27
Job 22.1–9, 21–30

To reflect on the relationship between community, God and individuals in times of hardship and suffering.

Way in

Begin by sharing Psalm 139.

● Are there experiences for which we would like to thank God today?

● Are there things that we feel sorry about?

● Are there experiences about which we feel angry with God?

● When do we feel angry with God?

● Is it God's fault?

A relationship that survives stress

Job's relationship with God is such that it includes criticism and anger as much as love and praise. Not all relationships have this capacity. Indeed, to witness this treatment, in a similar vein to Job, may well feel offensive and abusive.

Read Job 8.1–22, remembering that Job's sons were no angels: Job compensated for their uncouth behaviour, by making burnt offerings to God for their sanctification (1.4–6).

● How helpful is a relationship if it cannot bear the difficulties as well as the pleasures?

By chapter 13, Job's friends have tested him to the limit! They have been very condescending with him. They do not compromise. Their relationship is at a very low ebb. Job turns to his best friend, God, and vents all his frustration and anger on him.

Job refuses to accept human judgement. He knows that he is answerable to God. He is also sure that he is innocent.

● Does this remind us of some of the laments within the Psalms or of 20th century examples — of people held in detention, tortured for their faith, imprisoned without a fair trial? If you are not familiar with any of these, see some examples on pages 34–35.

Attitudes in the church community

● Job's friends wrongly assumed that Job's suffering was a result of sin. How prevalent is this idea even today?

● How easily does the community (the Church or people in the neighbourhood) respond to families/individuals in need —
— when a member of the household is ill?
— when disaster strikes the area — flood, fire or theft?
— when there is a national/international disaster?

● How easy is it for a Christian to admit that s/he is going through a hard patch?

● Are Christians sometimes afraid of their difficulties reflecting on their faith or on a member of a particular Church?

Adding to your model
What caption will you write on today's brick?

PRAYER

Lord, sometimes we feel sorry for Job
and yet so pleased for him that he remained firm to you.
Lord, sometimes we feel sorry for Job's friends

How easy is it for a Christian to admit that s/he is going through a hard patch?

who misread the situation so badly.
Lord, sometimes we feel sorry for ourselves,
for our faint-heartedness
and inability to remain firm in our convictions
whatever befalls.
Lord, sometimes we feel sorry for you:
you love us so much that you overlook all our weaknesses
and continue to love us.
And then we remember
that Job wasn't the only one who suffered,
for you took upon yourself the sufferings of the whole world
in order that the world might know and believe.
So thank you, Lord, for remaining firm for our sakes
and for building a community of disciples
who learned, with your help, how to build a Church.
Amen

Study 10 *God is with us*

AIM

To draw together this series of studies on building community, and to explore what we can learn from our suffering to strengthen community.

Way in

Take time to reflect on the previous nine studies of this theme, and reflect on how much they have made you aware of what builds a community.

● What are the difficulties? Or have you achieved a better perspective on the issues?

A happy ending?

In the later chapters of Job, God asks lots of questions and sets the whole story in a world context. For me God's answer has overtones of Psalm 8.

● Does the comparison speak to you?

● What have we to say to the following questions today?
— Source of our life, what are we?

—What is our life? What is our love?
—What is our justice? What is our success?
—What is our endurance? What is our power?
—What can we say before You?

Jewish Daily Prayer — Forms of Prayer Vol 1
(Reform Synagogues of Great Britain)

We do not know whether Job ever lived, and yet he feels so human, as do his 'friends'. This great poem from Hebrew tradition describes so much so graphically. Its characters come alive and speak to our own experience; it is timeless.

Perhaps the most unnatural part of the story is its ending. Like many other traditional stories, it has a happy ending. God makes all things well.

● Is it like that in real life? Do we expect it to be so?

● Can you think of other possible endings? How might they speak to our experience?

● Reflect on the story of Job in the light of what happened to the Son of God.

Suffering and community

Why end a series of studies on building community with a fairly detailed exploration of the book of Job?

1. Together list categories of people in your community whose suffering — e.g. blindness, learning disabilities... — makes them feel marginalized. By the side of each category, make a note of attempts being made today to affirm them and draw them into community.

2. Think of areas of the world where communities are currently going through a time of great suffering through political conflict, drought, flood, famine, epidemic... Again, make a list. Think of examples of how communities are getting together to tackle these problems. Think back to similar times in your own country's history, and recall how ordinary people responded to the crises.

3. One of the remarkable features of all these experiences, both the personal and the political/social ones, is that, in ways we may not be able to explain, people are drawn together in mutual support and rehabilitation.

Reflect on the story of Job in the light of what happened to the Son of God

With great resilience, new life comes out of the ashes of the old

With great resilience, new life comes out of the ashes of the old. And often Christians in those places have been heard to say, 'God is with us in the struggle.' Reflect together on this and share experiences.

Adding to your model

Your final caption on your last brick should now draw together what makes a community!

PRAYER

Encourage the group to think of:

● people who are perhaps misunderstood or misjudged in community...

● people who need comfort — the sick and dying, the old, people facing uncertainty...

● people who are comforters and listeners, mediators, people working towards reconciliation...

● communities in other parts of the world who are going through a time of great suffering...

...people like Job, whose lives have been tested and tried almost to the limits of human endurance.

Remember the communities represented by each member of the group. Pray for solidarity and courage, harmony and mutual understanding

Remember the communities represented by each member of the group. Pray for solidarity and courage, harmony and mutual understanding.

Remember this 'community' which meets each week. Commit each member into God's loving care.

Bless one another by sharing the Grace.

ACTION

Set up a graffiti board in a prominent place for next Sunday's worshippers. Write on it in large capitals the words, 'COMMUNITY IS...' and add phrases from the 'bricks' in large print and different colours around it. Invite people to add other words they think should be seen in relation to 'community'. Keep the board up for a few weeks, though not indefinitely!

VOICES OF CREATION

NOTES
BY
JOY MEAD

Study 1 *Celebration*

AIM

To explore and celebrate the joy at the heart of all creation.

Preparation:

If possible, have available examples of Celtic art, particularly tree of life designs representing the connectedness of all created life: plant, insect, fish, reptile, bird, animal and people.

Come prepared with something you have seen, experienced or hoped for during the past seven days and would like to celebrate with others. The form in which you bring this can be photo, story, artefact, gift...

Seeing God

The following extract is from Alice Walker's book *The Colour Purple*. It is a conversation between the abused and misused Celie and Shug Avery, singer and magic woman. Shug resurrects the joy of life in Celie and transforms her suffering into hope.

'Here's the thing, say Shug. The thing I believe. God is inside you and inside everybody else. You come into the world with God. But only them that search for it inside find it...

But what do it look like? I ast.

Don't look like nothing, she say. It ain't a picture show. It ain't something you can look at apart from anything else, including yourself. I believe God is everything, say Shug. Everything that is or ever was or ever will be. And when you can feel that, and be happy to feel that, you've found It.

Shug a beautiful something, let me tell you. She frown a little, look out cross the yard, lean back in her chair, look like a big rose.

She say, My first step from the old white man* was

Keynote readings
Psalm 104.1–23
Genesis 2.4b–25
Job 38.19–33
Job 39.13–30
Mark 4.26–34
Colossians 1.15–20

Celtic logo of the Iona Community

'Any fool living in the world can see it always trying to please us back'

Alice Walker, The Colour Purple

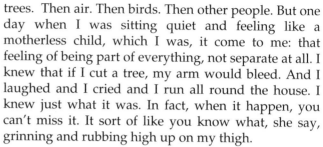

trees. Then air. Then birds. Then other people. But one day when I was sitting quiet and feeling like a motherless child, which I was, it come to me: that feeling of being part of everything, not separate at all. I knew that if I cut a tree, my arm would bleed. And I laughed and I cried and I run all round the house. I knew just what it was. In fact, when it happen, you can't miss it. It sort of like you know what, she say, grinning and rubbing high up on my thigh.

Shug! I say.

Oh, she say. God love all them feelings... God love everything you love — and a mess of stuff you don't... I think it pisses God off if you walk by the colour purple in a field somewhere and don't notice it.

What it do when it pissed off? I ast.

Oh it make something else. People think pleasing God is all God care about. But any fool living in the world can see it always trying to please us back.

...Yeah, she say. It always making little surprises and springing them on us when us least expect.

You mean it want to be loved, just like the bible say.

Yes, Celie, she say. Everything want to be loved...'

* Shug's first image of God

Alice Walker, The Colour Purple
(The Women's Press 1983)

Talk about the changes in Shug's image of God and the way this transforms her life. What does the story tell us about seeing, experiencing, hoping?

Read:

'In the late Middle Ages, the poets and singers of Scotland were known as Makars, 'makers'. It is not too fanciful to imagine the universe as the song of God the Makar, a joyous outpouring of energy and creativity and wild ordering and continuous exchanges. And it is truly a religious instinct to respond to God's song-making with our antiphon of praise. Creation makes worshippers of us.'

Kathy Galloway, Words for Today 2000 (IBRA)

The maker God

Make the things you have brought into a collage, perhaps adding words to make a Celebration Song — like the Celtic patterns, a joyful response to the maker God.

Towards a conclusion

...Maker of heaven and earth...
It is a good thing to be a maker.
Breadmaker, pounding breath into dough
on a flat stone;
cake-maker, for celebrations, or chocolate
for times of indulgent misery;
dressmaker, cutting, patterning, fashioning,
fitting to a shape;
toolmaker, the maker's makar;
love-maker, skill-sharing artisan of
pleasure, trust, delight;
baby-maker.

Wood and words, stone and steel,
clay, lace, brick, flower, flour, microchip —
whatever the medium
it is a good thing to be a maker.
Substantial,
material,
concrete,
the exchange of energies
changing the world.

It is a great thing to be a
maker of heaven and earth,
is it not?

> *From* Talking to the Bones, *Kathy Galloway*
> *(SPCK 1996)*

PRAYER

Colourful God of light and laughter
help us to dance our dreams into being...

ACTION

Have a party: celebrate together with poetry, music, singing, dancing, eating and drinking ... and go out with hope.

Study 2 *Protest*

Keynote readings
Genesis 3.1–4.16
Deuteronomy
28.15–24
Isaiah 24.1–13
Joel 1.1–20
Romans 8.18–22

AIM

To explore together how our search for scapegoats, and our refusal to acknowledge our own responsibility for the abuse of our earth and the life it supports, defuse protest and stand in the way of change.

Preparation
Ask people to come with newspaper or magazine cuttings of stories which reflect the search for scapegoats.

Looking for scapegoats
Read Genesis 3.1–13.

This is a popular passage. Why do you think that is? Is it something to do with our tendency to look for scapegoats?

Ask each member of the group to present his or her own version or re-telling of the story, perhaps with the help of newspaper cuttings. Who are the present-day scapegoats: single mothers, beggars, asylum seekers...? Talk about your stories.

'I did eat the apple. It is my responsibility. I cannot blame anyone else. The responsibility for the knowledge and the way the knowledge is used is mine'

From Silence in Heaven

Whose responsibility?
Ask a woman in the group to read the following extract from a sermon by Janet Lees in which she speaks as Eve.

I accept responsibility for eating the apple. I ate the apple. I wanted the knowledge. I wanted to become wise. I accept the responsibility for the knowledge. It wasn't all I thought it would be; there was knowledge of good things. There was also knowledge of bad things. There was knowledge of joy and happiness but also knowledge of pain and suffering. At first it wasn't easy to accept responsibility for all this knowledge, I wanted to blame someone else. I blamed the snake, saying I'd been tricked. It was easier to blame someone else than accept the responsibility myself. I wanted to hide from this new responsibility, this new wisdom. So I blamed someone else. But I did eat the apple. It is my responsibility. I cannot blame anyone else. The responsibility for the knowledge and the way the knowledge is used is mine. I ate the apple. I ate the apple!

From Silence in Heaven, *a book of women's preaching*
edited by Heather Walton and Susan Durber
(SCM Press 1994)

Keep a few moments' silence.

Then think about how we come into the world: good but capable of creative or destructive choices.

Talk about interconnectedness and the responsibility choice brings. Do we, for example, choose not to understand the connections between the cars we drive and dying trees or children with asthma? Between bulging supermarket shelves in one place and deepening hunger in another?

● Are we prepared to talk about charity but not to talk about money, the distribution of wealth, our freedom to choose not to exploit?

● Do we see remaining silent as a choice?

Towards a conclusion

A child, a woman and a man
are people in a foreign land,
whose word I doubt, whose hopes I fear,
whose ways I cannot understand,
and yet I need to feel and know
how Christ my Saviour, knows and loves
that very woman, child and man.

For if I somehow shift the blame
for all my fear and guilt within,
the foreigners I cannot love
will be the scapegoats for my sin,
as they look evil, I feel good,
and in the name of Christ destroy
the work of Christ and feel no shame.

Brian Wren, Piece Together Praise
(Stainer & Bell)

Do we choose not to understand the connections between the cars we drive and dying trees or children with asthma? Between bulging supermarket shelves in one place and deepening hunger in another?

PRAYER

God of our freedom,
give us informed minds
and warm hearts
so that we are ready
to protest or proclaim
and live as those blessed
not blamed. Amen

Many groups protest at the exploitation of the earth and its creatures and celebrate wholeness. Contact Friends of the Earth or One World Week to find out more. Include the whole earth — all living things — in your thinking and prayers.

Study 3 *Call for Action*

Keynote readings

Leviticus 25.1–34
1 Kings 21.1–27
Isaiah 1.2–9, 15–20
Micah 6.6–8

Forgiving debt is Sabbath activity: it's letting go control and giving a poor person a new start; it's letting people who know what is good for them become the people they want to be rather than the people we want them to be

AIM

To explore the way in which a call to action can be more about letting go and letting be than doing.

Way in

Write on a large sheet of paper words people associate with Sunday or Sabbath. Look at the words together and begin to think about our Sabbath selves — who we are when we're not doing. Look carefully at the being words.

Sabbath and Jubilee

Read together Leviticus 25.1–12.

Talk about the links between Sabbath and Jubilee. What has been done in the name of progress has often been so harmful that maybe we now need to learn to do less. Think about times when not everything that could be done should be done. The horn of Jubilee sounds for a pause to think and allow healing to take place.

Forgiving debt is Sabbath activity: it's letting go control and giving a poor person a new start; it's letting people who know what is good for them become the people they want to be rather than the people we want them to be.

How?

Consider the following words:

'The poor do not want you to impose your programmes to empower us. We know how to empower ourselves. We want your support for our decisions.'

Karuawathie Menike,
People's Rural Development Association, Sri Lanka
(The New Internationalist, *March 1999*)

'To the country's leaders I say: give us back our voice,

you have stolen it. Give us back our dignity and allow us the tools with which to help ourselves.'

The UK Coalition Against Poverty
(The New Internationalist, *March 1999*)

Talk about what this means in terms of the activities of rich countries, rich people and the concept of growth as it applies to those who control.

● Do we need to look again at our values?
● What sort of growth is needed?

Reflection

Read:

The Contented Fisherman

The rich industrialist from the north was horrified to find the Southern fisherman lying lazily beside his boat, smoking a pipe.

'Why aren't you out fishing?' said the industrialist.

'Because I have caught enough fish for the day,' said the fisherman.

'Why don't you catch some more?'

'What would I do with it?'

'You could earn more money' was the reply.

'With that you could have a motor fixed to your boat and go into deeper waters and catch more fish. Then you would make enough to buy nylon nets. These would bring you more fish and more money. Soon you would have enough money to own two boats ... maybe even a fleet of boats. Then you would be a rich man like me.'

'What would I do then?'

'Then you could really enjoy life.'

'What do you think I am doing right now?'

From The Song of the Bird *by Anthony de Mello*
(Doubleday)

Think about life as a cycle, seasons, mysteries, celebrations. Have we tried to make it something different — a 70-year economic plan perhaps?

Look at the deeper implications of the story and its links with the piece from Leviticus. Think about life as a cycle, seasons, mysteries, celebrations. Have we tried to make it something different — a 70-year economic plan perhaps?

Towards a conclusion

Perhaps what matters is not so much what we do but what we dream of and long for ... and if we dare to meet the longing of our hearts.

PRAYER

God of our longing:
may we
begin to understand
that just to be
is a blessing;
just to live
is holy.
May we
enjoy the earth gently
for once it is spoiled
there will be nothing
for us to do
but weep.

ACTION

Next time you meet someone for the first time stop and think about the holiness of his/her being — as well as about the work s/he does.

Next time you meet someone for the first time stop and think about the holiness of his/her being — as well as about the work s/he does.

Study 4 *Hope*

Keynote readings
Psalm 146
Isaiah 11.1–9
Joel 2.18–27
Zechariah 8.1–13
Mark 4.1–9
Hebrews 9.24–28
Revelation 22.1–5

AIM

To look at seeds of hope: the way they are sown and nurtured; the way they endure and transform.

Way in

Talk about images of hope. Books like *Dear Life* (Christian Aid) have some good examples. Think about what keeps folk in desperately poor situations dreaming of a better future. Compare these images with the imagery used in advertising to arouse expectation and create a need (or a greed?).

● What are the most popular words?

● How do expectation words and hope words compare?

Seeds of hope
Read together Mark 4.1–9.

Interpret this story using role-play. There are many ways of using the ideas of seed, growth and transformation from the original story. Use as many as you can. Think about the vulnerability of seeds, their fragility and their strength: the same seeds, with different results when planted in different soils. Concentrate on hope as you look again at the yield in the story and think about what this really means.

Talk about your stories and the mystery and creativity of story-telling. By extension this parable is about different responses that might be made to any story. Hope is often telling stories and letting them sow seeds in the fertile soil of human imagination. A single living seed can grow and spread across acres of human minds. It will generate many responses within the mind's unfailing capacity for wonder. Once the seed is planted the story-teller can be silent, letting the imagination of the world provide the fertile soil.

Once the seed is planted the story-teller can be silent, letting the imagination of the world provide the fertile soil

Read this piece as a meditation:
... in the dying of autumn, I see the birthing of spring.
God is kind. This is the way of the kingdom.
So I surrender myself to the movement of life,
to the hand of God.

I look at my own hand. It is closed, still clutching for what is gone.
But I cannot scatter seed with a clenched fist.
I open my hand. I let go of all that I have been holding that needs to die.
It hurts to let it go. But it is the hurt of life.
Now I can sow new seed.

My seeds are small. But they have great potential.
I don't know where they will take root.
So I want to sow well, with care;
seeds of friendship and respect, and value for people.
Seeds of justice and love.
Seeds of reverence and encouragement.

How might repentance bring hope for rich people and nations?

I want to sow seeds of peace.

I can only sow.
For the rest, I trust, and I let go.

Kathy Galloway, Talking to the Bones *(SPCK)*

● How much of hope is about letting go?

● How might repentance bring hope for rich people and nations?

Towards a conclusion

The precious seed of life is in our keeping,

yet if we plant it, and fulfil our trust,

tomorrow's sun will rise on joy and weeping,

and shine upon the unjust and the just.

Our calling is to live our human story

of good and bad, achievement, love and loss,

then hand it on to future shame or glory,

lit by our hope, and leavened by the cross.

Come, let us guard the gateway to existence,

that thousands yet may stand where we have stood,

give thanks for life and, praising our persistence,

enjoy this lovely earth, and call it good.

Brian Wren, Piece Together Praise
(Stainer and Bell)

PRAYER

God, who is the quivering voice of new life in all creation, may we sow seeds of love and hope in our hearts and water them with our tears.

ACTION

Find out more about Christian Aid's *Partners for Change* which aims to give people the means to achieve their own dreams.

Study 5 *Prayer*

AIM

To encourage a sense of immediacy and wonder; to enhance our understanding of prayer as giving loving attention.

Preparation

Have ready:

● *one large candle and smaller ones for each member of the group, or ask each member to bring a candle (and don't forget to prepare somewhere to stand them);*

● *a large sheet of paper.*

Lighting a candle

Light the large candle and contemplate it silently for a short while.

Reflect together:

Lighting a candle is a prayer. When you have gone it stays alight. Its glow lights up a little space, illuminates hiddenness and mystery, becomes a symbol of love and hope, light and warmth. It kindles your personal prayers in the hearts and minds of others so that there is community and connectedness.

People light candles when a child dies, when a friend is ill, when a neighbour loses her job... The candle is more than itself: it becomes: comfort for the mourning, healing for the sick, self-respect for the rejected ... a garden full of sunflowers or the touch of a lover ... the yes of a breath of fresh air... It is a way of letting go.

Silently light each individual candle from the large one. Think about the moment of lighting; how one flame can be lit from another without diminishing it; what matters in each wish or intention.

Talk about doing this. Can you see the candle as a parable — story as well as symbol? Remain silent for a while then ask each one to express what his or her candle has become. Try to shape these into a poem.

Biblical reflection

Read together: Psalm 65.

Keynote readings

1 Samuel 1.4–20
1 Samuel 2.1–10
1 Samuel 3.1–21
Isaiah 42.14–20
Psalm 65
Psalm 84
Hebrews 10.11–14
2 Samuel 23.1–7
Jeremiah 2.1–13
Jeremiah 10.12–16
Jeremiah 12.1–13
Jereniah 18.1–12
Daniel 7.9–10, 13–14
Revelation 1.4b–8

We long for a candle of the spirit to show hidden things; we long for perception to enable us to hear the sounds of the earth. We long for connectedness

We long for a candle of the spirit to show hidden things; we long for perception to enable us to hear the sounds of the earth. We long for connectedness. Lighting a candle can be an expression of these longings.

Look again at verse 13 of the Psalm. This is about one of the myriad 'voices' of creation. Talk together about times when you have heard the 'voice' of creation.

Now read this poem together:

Stones and Rainbows — a poetry reading on Iona

At this bright edge of the world
a dancing light plays on stones
and wind overlays them
like a fine cloth.

All along the shore
I can feel their scattered presence
the way they hold colours;
mottled and marbled;
the way they hoard secrets,
not passive but still;
knowing they will be
in at the end.

In the evening we are waiting
amid the Abbey's upsurging stones;
for poetry
when the rainbow comes —
a surprise every time —
and frees our hearts
to cry
Today, Today.   *Joy Mead*

● What do you think creation is saying here?
● What is being illuminated?

Towards a conclusion

Live slowly, think slowly, for time is a mystery,
Never forget that love
Requires always that you be
The greatest person you are capable of being.

Be grateful for the manifold
Dreams of creation
And the many ways of the unnumbered peoples.

Be grateful for life as you live it.
And may a wonderful light
Always guide you on the unfolding road.

> Ben Okri, 'To an English Friend in Africa'
> *in* An African Elegy, *Ben Okri*
> *(Jonathan Cape, 1992)*

PRAYER

Help us, Hidden God
to see ordinary things
in holy light;
and to hear the heartbeat
of our good earth. Amen

ACTION

Try to make your life a prayer by living fully in the light and wonder of each given moment and attending with care and gentleness to the humblest things.

Try to make your life a prayer by living fully in the light and wonder of each given moment and attending with care and gentleness to the humblest things

NOTES
BY
KATE HUGHES

ADVENT —
GOD IS WITH US

Study 1 *God's Kingdom*

Keynote readings
Matthew 5.3–7
Matthew 5.8–12
1 Thessalonians 3.9–1

*Is this really
what Advent is
about?*

AIM
To look at the purpose of Advent and its relevance for our lives.

Way in
Advent has just begun. Discuss with the group what their lives will be like for the next four weeks. Extra busy? Extra tiring? More to do at home? More work? More shopping? Special events at church? More activities to fit in with their children (school plays, concerts, bazaars, etc.)? More eating and drinking?

● Is this picture of hyper-activity really what Advent is about?

● Why does the Church give us these four weeks before Christmas as a special season?

● What are we preparing for/looking forward to?

We are looking forward to the final coming of God's Kingdom, and the annual reminder that Jesus has already come as the 'Yes' to all God's promises *(2 Corinthians 1.20).*

The coming of the Kingdom
What is the Kingdom like? Look at the key readings together and make a list of the characteristics of the Kingdom.

● How do our Advent activities compare with the life of the Kingdom?

● How much do they contribute to the coming of the Kingdom?

Reflect together on the following comment:

'The Kingdom, it seems to me, is always a dynamic, sudden, unpredictable happening. It can be an unexpected radical appearance of some Kingdom value. It can be the appearance of some activity or people which only makes sense in the light of the Kingdom. It can be the manifestation of some new reality that reverses the expectations of background, environment, culture or history. Inevitably we say, 'Lo, here' — 'by the grace of God, lo here'. But then we cannot build on it, much less can we 'build the Kingdom'. But we can prepare for it, service it, and celebrate its appearing.'

John Vincent, Words for Today 2000 *(IBRA)*

PRAYER

O God, you know how busy Advent can be —
So many extra things to fit in,
So many people asking for our attention and our help.
You know, too, how lonely Advent can be —
When no one seems to want us
Or need our gifts or our help.
Show us how to focus more on you,
On the wonder of your love,
On the promise of your Kingdom,
So that in the midst of busyness
Or loneliness
We may find you
And be found by you. Amen

ACTION

Decide together on one activity for Advent to prepare for the coming of God's Kingdom, or to make you better instruments to bring it about. For example:

● read a book;

● give more time to prayer;

● be still for a few minutes every day;

● switch off by going for a walk;

● use a Christian Advent calendar with your children;

● make simple Christmas presents instead of buying expensive gifts;

Be still for a few minutes every day

117

● join a choir practising Christmas hymns/songs;

● stop doing something, so that life is less hectic.

Or — think up a Kingdom action to do in your own neighbourhood this Christmas. Find out the facts: who is in need, who would help, what you could do. For example, find out who will have no Christmas Day dinner, and plan a way to deal with the problem *(suggested in* Words for Today 2000*).*

Study 2 *God is with us*

Keynote reading
Luke 1.5–46

AIM

To enter into the reality of Mary's preparation for the coming of Jesus.

Preparation
You will need at least one picture of the Nativity — perhaps a painting by an Old Master, or paintings of the Nativity by artists of different cultures.

Growth takes time

Discuss times when members of the group have agreed to take on new work, or extra responsibilities. How did it feel? Did you get it right immediately, or did you have to 'grow into it'? Who gave you help and support?

The idealized picture

How do you think Mary really felt?

Mary is often portrayed in words and pictures as responding serenely and effortlessly to the message of the angel. But was it really like that? God was asking Mary to become pregnant before marriage and to give birth to a boy who was not the son of the man she was about to marry. And her son was not going to be any ordinary boy, either. Before the birth, she had to go on a journey, and ended up giving birth to him in a stable.

Pass round a picture of the nativity, perhaps a painting by an Old Master.

● How realistic do you think the scene is?

● If you have more than one painting, reflect together on the differences.

Read Luke 1.5–46. In pairs discuss the following

questions:

- How do you think Mary really felt?
- Why do you think Mary decided to visit Elizabeth?
- What was the result of that visit?
- How do you think Joseph felt?

Come together and share your thoughts.

Mary, like everyone else, had to grow into her new responsibilities. What helped her was her certainty that if God asks us to do something, he will provide the grace to enable us to obey. This grace may come from the situation itself, through other people, or by the direct action of the Holy Spirit — but it will be there when we need it.

Look again at verses 46–55. What else does this great song tell us about the character and person of Mary?

PRAYER

Lord, change can be scary.
New work, new responsibilities,
New neighbours, new babies,
New relationships, new skills —
They can be exciting
But they can also make us feel inadequate.
Help us to remember
That if they are your will for us
You will be with us as you were with Mary,
Helping us to grow into change
And sending people to help and support us. Amen

Allow time to think of people who are facing new situations, and pray for them silently.

ACTION

Either individually, or as a group, think of people known to you who are facing new situations (work, home, baby, relationship, illness, etc.). What can you do to support them? Pray for them regularly? Visit or phone them? Send a card? Help in practical ways?

For next week

Ask the group to bring some old Christmas cards, or some cards that they have already received this year.

Study 3 *God's judgement and promise*

Keynote reading
Luke 1.5–46

AIM

To renew our trust in God's promises, as they are demonstrated in the coming of Christ.

Preparation

You will need:

● *scissors, glue and pens/pencils of various colours;*

● *rectangles of paper (for each member of the group) approximately 18cm by 16cm.*

The promise of Christmas

Encourage the group to think of recent examples of injustice, evil and oppression. Then think of similar news of justice and goodness.

Jesus is the 'Yes' pronounced upon God's promises

Christmas is a time for facing up to the fact that 2,000 years of Christianity don't seem to have made much difference in the world. Yet Christianity is a religion of 'now' and 'not yet'. God's Kingdom and rule are now, but the perfection of the Kingdom is still to come. The promise of Christmas is that God's Kingdom will come. God's promises will be fulfilled. Jesus is the 'Yes' pronounced upon God's promises *(2 Corinthians 1.20)*.

The promises of God

Read the keynote reading. What does God promise in it?

Ask each person to show the Christmas cards they have brought and to read out the greetings printed inside. Ask each member to say which greeting best sums up the real promise of Christmas, and to explain why.

A Christmas greeting

Give each person one of the card rectangles you have prepared and ask them to make a Christmas card. Either draw a picture (it can be very simple), or cut out and mount an appropriate image from old cards. Underneath or inside write a greeting which gives the true meaning of Christmas.

PRAYER

Peace, happiness,
All the best, season's greetings,
Joy, merry Christmas,
Prosperity, good wishes...
So many different greetings for Christmas.
Yet only one word
Needs to be said:
Emmanuel
God is with us.
Thank you, God,
For the wonder of your Christmas word to us. Amen

ACTION

- Take your card to someone who is lonely. Spend some time with him or her and if appropriate include a time of prayer.
- Or display your card at home and use it as a focus for meditation for the rest of Advent.

For next week

Next week's activity involves making a crib scene. You will need: a cardboard box, cardboard tubes, wire or pipe cleaners, scraps of material, plasticine or Blu-tack, glue, paints...

Study 4 *Come and worship*

AIM

To help members of the group to welcome all people to the worship of God.

The Christmas crib

The crib reminds us that from Day One Jesus lived an unusual life. He was born, not in a house, but in an outhouse. His temporary first home had more in common with shop doorways where the homeless sleep in our big cities than with the comfortable homes in which many of his followers live today. As we saw when we looked at Christmas cards last week, the reality of Jesus' birth is not

Emmanuel
God is with us

Keynote reading
Luke 2.1–20

How can we provide alternative accommodation?

always recognized. The stables look too clean and cosy. Jesus was born in alternative accommodation, and in his life welcomed many others who had been pushed aside by 'normal' and respectable society. Ask the group to make a list: the homeless, the disreputable, those needing healing, those needing God's (and our) generosity, those needing practical service, those needing peace and harmony in their lives.

Who comes to the crib today?

● Today, who needs the alternative accommodation offered by the stable?

● How can we, the Church, welcome those in need? How can we offer warmth, food, temporary shelter, friendship, support, a listening ear, prayer, the opportunity to draw closer to and worship God...?

In pairs, think about people you know who need to be welcomed on behalf of Jesus (be careful to preserve their anonymity and not slip into gossip!).

Making a crib

In southern France, each village produces its own Christmas crib. Round the family of Mary, Joseph and the baby stand a crowd of little figures — the mayor, the postman, the butcher, the baker, the priest, the schoolteacher — representing the life of the village being brought into the presence of Christ.

According to the abilities of the group, make your own crib, drawing or making figures to represent all those in your own community who need to be specially welcomed to the stable.

PRAYER

We cannot literally take people by the hand and lead them into the presence of the new-born Jesus. But as the continuing Body of Christ, we can show them the love and compassion and challenge of Christ, so that they will want to know him more and worship him:

Christ has no body now on earth but yours,

No hands but yours,

No feet but yours.

Yours are the eyes through which is to look out Christ's compassion for the world,
Yours are the feet with which he is to go about doing good,
Yours are the hands with which he is to bless people now. Amen

St Teresa of Avila (1515–82)

ACTION

Who are today's homeless (either physically or spiritually), or disreputable shepherds, or people in need of healing, generosity, service and peace? What can we as a group do to identify one or more such visitor to the stable and make them feel more welcome in the local community and in our church?

Yours are the eyes through which is to look out Christ's compassion for the world

APPENDIX

Answer to the puzzle on page 40:

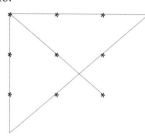

Answers to the exercise on page 53:

1. 'Hear, O Israel, the Lord is our God, one Lord, and you must love the Lord your God with all your heart and mind and soul and strength.'

   Judaism — the Shema — from Deuteronomy 6

2. 'He alone is pure whose heart is pure.'

   Sikhism — words of Guru Nanak

3. 'Anger must be overcome by the absence of anger;
   Evil must be overcome by good;
   Greed must be overcome by liberality;
   Lies must be overcome by truth.'

   Buddhism — from the Dhammapada

4. 'You must not retaliate when another does you injury.'

   Hinduism — from the Ramayana

5. 'In the city joyful dwell all the saints of God. Neither suffering nor sorrow is found there.'

   Sikhism — from the Ravidas

6. 'He will not enter hell, who has faith equal to a grain of mustard seed in his heart.'

Islam — words of Mohammed

7. 'You shall not seek revenge, or cherish anger towards your kinsfolk; you shall love your neighbour as a man like yourself. I am the Lord.'

Judaism — from Leviticus 19

8. 'Thou who stealest the hearts of those that love thee, drown me in the sea of Thy love.'

Hinduism — from a Bengali hymn

9. 'The Divine Mercy is perfect, in the sense that it answers every need. It is universal in the sense that it spreads alike over those who merit it and those who do not merit it.'

Islam — words of Al-Ghazali

10. 'From the unreal lead me to the real;
From darkness lead me to light;
From death lead me to immortality.'

Hinduism

11. 'If someone has done you wrong, do not repay him with a wrong.'

Christian — from Romans 12

12. 'He who gladly accepts the suffering of this world brings salvation to the world.'

Judaism — words of Rabbi Joshua ben Levi

IBRA prayer books compiled by Maureen Edwards

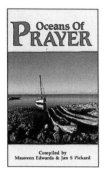

Oceans of Prayer

(Compiled by Maureen Edwards and Jan S Pickard)
This collection of prayers arises out of the depths of a wide variety of experiences from different parts of the world. Their voices mingle in praise of our common Lord and in intercession for the world in which we live.
We seek God's presence, we praise and thank him, we pray for ourselves and for others and, as we meditate, we reflect on his word.

£5.00

Living Prayers for Today

A collection of prayers which has already become an essential book both for private devotions and for public worship. It gathers together well-known prayers of the past with prayers of today from different parts of the world. *Living Prayers for Today* contains prayers for all occasions, and is designed to be user-friendly for individuals, groups and churches.

£13.00

More Living Prayers for Today

This anthology, a companion volume to *Living Prayers for Today*, focuses on the Christian festivals and includes some prayers for everyday use. It expresses a strong sense of God's love for the world and each person in it.
'A prayer from Sri Lanka speaks of water falling on dry tea-leaves and bringing out their flavour — many of the prayers in this book did that for me!'
  Baroness Kathleen Richardson OBE,
  Moderator, Free Church Federal Council

£13.00

Order through your IBRA Representative or from the appropriate address on page 128.

Our partners overseas

The IBRA International Fund, available through the generous donations of many readers, helps Christian organizations in developing countries to produce their own Bible reading notes. Some are reproduced in English, but most are translated and printed locally. In many cases we supply the book covers and the film ready for printing. Sometimes we supply the text and a grant towards local production, thus helping to provide local employment as well as encouragement to read the Bible regularly.

Bible reading cards giving the daily texts are translated into several languages and distributed, usually without charge, to many parts of the world.

It is difficult to estimate the exact number of people reading the daily Bible passages throughout the world, but it may be in excess of half a million.

In Christian service

IBRA has been serving the World Church since 1882. Now, at the beginning of a new millennium, we look to the future with renewed vision and enthusiasm to provide the necessary means to enable the Church worldwide to meet some of its publishing and resources needs.

As the Christian world opens up, communities responding to the Christian message need books and resources to learn and understand. These are often too expensive in the developing world, which is why the International Fund of IBRA — A Really Bright Idea! — needs your help.

Help us to increase the number of people regularly reading the Bible through our Bible reading notes and cards, by:

● Giving generously — speak to your IBRA Representative or write to the appropriate address on page 128 for details of covenants, donations and legacies. The only money we have to use is the money you give.

● Praying for all who are involved in the work of IBRA, both in the UK and overseas.

INTERNATIONAL BIBLE READING ASSOCIATION

– a worldwide service of the National Christian Education Council
at work in five continents.

HEADQUARTERS

1020 Bristol Road
Selly Oak
Birmingham
Great Britain
B29 6LB
and the following agencies

AUSTRALIA

Uniting Education (previously The Joint Board of Christian Education)
PO Box 1245 (65 Oxford Street)
Collingwood
Victoria 3066

GHANA

IBRA Secretary
PO Box 919
Accra

INDIA

All India Sunday School Association
PO Box 2099
Secunderabad – 500 003
Andhra Pradesh

NEW ZEALAND

Epworth Bookshop
PO Box 6133, Te Aro
75 Taranaki Street
Wellington 6035

NIGERIA

IBRA Representative
PMB 5298
Ibadan

SOUTH AND CENTRAL AFRICA

IBRA Representative
Box 1176
Sedgefield 6573